THE EMOTIONAL GROWTH
OF TEENS

Other Books by William L. Fibkins

Wake Up Counselors! Restoring Counseling Services for Troubled Teens

Class Warfare: Focus on "Good" Students Is Ruining Schools

Angel Teachers: Educators Who Care about Troubled Teens

Stopping the Brain Drain of Skilled Veteran Teachers: Retaining and Valuing their Hard-Won Experience

An Administrator's Guide to Better Teacher Mentoring, 2nd Edition

Teen Obesity: How Schools Can Be the Number One Solution to the Problem

Innocence Denied: A Guide to Preventing Sexual Misconduct by Teachers and Coaches

Students in Trouble: Schools Can Help Before Failure

An Educator's Guide to Understanding the Personal Side of Students' Lives

An Administrator's Guide to Better Teacher Mentoring

THE EMOTIONAL GROWTH OF TEENS

How Group Counseling Intervention Works for Schools

William L. Fibkins

ROWMAN & LITTLEFIELD
Lanham • Boulder • New York • Toronto • Plymouth, UK

Published by Rowman & Littlefield
4501 Forbes Boulevard, Suite 200, Lanham, Maryland 20706
www.rowman.com

10 Thornbury Road, Plymouth PL6 7PP, United Kingdom

British Library Cataloguing in Publication Information Available

Library of Congress Cataloging-in-Publication Data

Library of Congress Cataloging-in-Publication Data Available

ISBN 978-1-4758-0719-6 (pbk. : alk. paper)—ISBN 978-1-4758-0720-2 (electronic)

♾™ The paper used in this publication meets the minimum requirements of American National Standard for Information Sciences Permanence of Paper for Printed Library Materials, ANSI/NISO Z39.48-1992.

Printed in the United States of America

CONTENTS

Preface   vii

Introduction   xi

1   Counseling Groups in Secondary Schools: The Need, Resistance, and Opportunity   1

2   Why Group Counseling Is an Important Strategy for Guidance and Counseling Programs   11

3   What Does a Model Group Counseling Program Look Like?   25

4   The First Step in Readying Counselors As Group Leaders: Listening to Their Concerns   41

5   Training Counselors As Group Leaders   65

6   Conclusion   101

References   109

PREFACE

I wrote this book out of my concern for the growing lack of personal counseling for students and because group counseling interventions can go a long way to restore this important service.

I have over thirty years of experience as a counselor, guidance director, founder of a student assistance program, counselor educator, and trainer and consultant to help schools reorganize their guidance and counseling programs. Given this experience I have observed a profession in trouble and counselors becoming more like administrators rather than offering the personal counseling that is a hallmark of their role.

For example, I have observed the rapid increase in counselors and guidance and counseling departments being used primarily to provide guidance and administrative activities such as overseeing mandated testing programs, scheduling of students for classes, data gathering, and college admissions, discipline, and attendance counseling.

As a result the personal counseling role of counselors in many schools has been demoted to a service in name only. While many school public relations publications herald the district's efforts to not let one student fall between the cracks, my experience is many students in need of personal counseling often find the counselor's door closed when they need help.

In many cases this is not the fault of counselors. They, like their students who need personal counseling, are victims of forces and the pressures they exert to make sure the counselor's role in today's secondary schools is to get students into a name college or the right classes, pass standardized tests, and limit discipline and attendance problems.

This role is one in which the counselor is also the gatherer of data to help the administrative staff paint a positive picture of both the students' and the school's successes and pass school budgets. This changing role of counselors should not come as a surprise. Administrators are under great pressure to gather positive information and good news about their school to win over critics.

As a result counselors have become the key players in assembling this information. The pressure is on them to deliver the good news needed by administrators to say, "Our students and staff are doing an outstanding job, here's the data." And the pressure is on counselors from college admissions directors to funnel students into their schools, especially with colleges struggling to survive. In my observation the counselor is being used as a salesperson for the school, not a personal counselor for kids in need.

Many of my recent books, such as *Wake Up, Counselors: Restoring Counseling Services for Troubled Teens*, *Class Warfare: Focus On "Good Students" Is Ruining Schools*, and *Angel Teachers: Educators Who Care about Troubled Teens*, have been written to demonstrate that alternatives are available to add more personal counseling for students and restore "counseling" services to guidance and counseling departments.

This new book is an effort to show counselors, directors of guidance and counseling, district student service administrators, and counselor educators how it is indeed possible and desirable to redesign their services to include group counseling; an outreach model which enables counselors to reach many more troubled students than they could utilizing the one-on-one counseling model, which is often the model used by counselors.

As this book outlines, adding a group counseling program can be accomplished by identifying a counselor well trained and skilled in group leadership to take on this role full time, provide one-on-one counseling as a backup to his group work, and train teachers, administrators, support staff, students, and parents who live and serve on the frontlines in the school and community as helpers. These helpers can serve as the eyes and ears of the program to identify and refer students headed for the margins of school and community life.

This personal counselor model can help bring about a positive bifurcation of guidance and counseling departments into two important parts and branches that work closely together. For example, a guidance branch in which counselors with administrative skills are focused on mandated testing programs, scheduling students for classes, data gathering, and college admissions, discipline, and attendance counseling and a counseling branch in which counselors are focused on interventions such as group and one-on-one counseling to help students resolve their personal problems.

As a result both branches are given equal priority and value in the school organization and personal counseling is no longer an afterthought. An added plus will be counselors with an administrative bent interested in offering guidance activities and counselors skilled and interested in offering personal counseling will finally be able to live amicably as professional partners.

I feel the approach called for in this book is unique, as it answers the question raised by many caring counselors: "How can we help more troubled kids when we are drowning in administrative tasks?" Rather than spending their professional lives asking the same question while stuck in an organizational wasteland, they can proceed to change the question of "how can we help" to the statement of "here's how we can help."

This book is organized around the following themes: a discussion of the present lack of group counseling interventions in our schools; reasons group counseling programs are important and can help resolve the personal problems of students; what a model group counseling program looks like; a training program for potential group leaders; and the opportunities and advantages personal counseling interventions can offer counselors and the guidance and counseling profession.

This book offers counselors and their profession a new life as a vital service for kids in need and a new helping role for caring educators, administrators, support staff, students, and parents. It trains them how to be their brother's keeper rather than onlookers who say "I am not qualified," or "it's not my job" and walk away, missing an opportunity to make a difference in helping a student in distress and in the process themselves.

In the end the major goal of this book is to help counselors, directors of guidance and counseling, and student service administrators move away from the old argument and way of thinking that says the only way to reach out to more at-risk students is to hire more counselors. In the majority of school districts that's not going to happen in the foreseeable future. New ways, models, and organizations need to be brought on line using existing staff in new ways to meet the growing needs of troubled students arriving at the school house door each day. This book offers doable new ideas and action plans.

INTRODUCTION

Group counseling intervention is one of the best ways to maximize counseling resources to reach more troubled teens. While there are other weapons in the counselor's arsenal, such as one-on-one counseling, group work is ideally suited to reach many more students, many who are experiencing common problems. Plus, there is another benefit when counselors offer group interventions. Often, when high school and junior high school students get help with their problems in groups, they want to be part of an effort to be involved in the school's helping outreach themselves. So, if properly encouraged, these potential leaders can be trained as peer counselors and added to the outreach offered by counselors.

This is a nuts and bolts story of the specific steps involved in developing a group program that is heralded by students, parents, school staff, administrators, and counselors and supported by them. It is not an intervention to be used only when a crisis hits the school, such as a suicide of a student, but rather a supported, ongoing, sought-after practice.

This book will reveal the good practices of group counseling for counselors in training, counselors, building principles, directors of counseling and guidance services, school district student services administrators, and counselor educators. The following good practices are needed by group counselors if they and their students are to be successful:

- The group counselor knows the students in his school well.
- In a variety of personal interactions and communications with students he signals he is interested in their world and issues, available for help if and when needed, and easily accessible. He sells himself and the variety of interventions, such as group counseling, he can offer. He is the go-to guy for help.
- He assesses the kinds of problems the students in his school are encountering and what kinds of group interventions would help.
- He enlists a network of "the eyes and ears of the school" such as administrators, teachers, support staff, counselors, student leaders, clerical staff, coaches, bus drivers, and community and parent advocates to refer students who are in trouble or heading for trouble. He affirms and acknowledges their critical role in the school's helping system; it "can't be done without them," he says! He holds regular meetings with his network to get their input and ideas. They are a team and must feel needed and involved.
- He develops an ongoing venue of groups to serve students with different needs and problems in the school. For example, using the author's own work at Shoreham-Wading River High School on Long Island, New York, as a model, organizing groups around such topics as how to handle pressure for high-achieving students and avoid addiction to "good grade pills"; health issues such as obesity and anorexia; addictions such as smoking, drinking, or drug-taking; teens on the road to dropping out; and a forty-eight-hour group to help troubled students get through their high-risk weekend.
- In the process of planning group interventions to meet the needs of groups and individuals in the school, he sells information about these groups with a variety of personal and written communications, enlisting his "eyes and ears of the school" network to make sure his outreach messages reaches every student, along with information on how to join these groups.
- One of his most prized skills is to sell what he has to offer to students, staff, administrators, parents, and community members so that they understand how and why this intervention effort is important to the schools and community. He is a salesperson for change and understands he operates in a very political and fluid arena which requires the support of many different constituencies. He knows good ideas and intentions in a new project die early on without political support.

- He offers ongoing training in the helping process to his network of "eyes and ears" members—administrators, staff, students, parents, and community leaders who serve on the frontlines of the school and community.
- He chronicles the kinds of problems students face in the school and which interventions appear to work and which do not for school administrators, teacher leaders, and community advocates.
- He understands why intervention systems need regular assessments and tune-ups to meet the needs of today's students and avoid the stagnation and failure that emerge with outdated systems. These systems fail both the students and the professionals who are trying to help them.

Group counseling programs require a number of steps in order to work and be successful. Finding and training a skilled group leader from the counseling staff is, of course, the first major step. This should be a person who has the motivation, courage, thick skin, will to win, determination, and willingness/ability to take the risks that are needed to nurture the program through the ups and downs that accompany the planning and implementation of the program. Show time, going live, and casting the program as a very professional, needed, and timely endeavor requires not only counseling skills but also political, salesmanship, public relations, and team-building skills.

Of course, there are very few human beings, nevermind counselors, who possess all of these attributes and skills. In order to find and prepare the "right" counselor for this role, directors of guidance and counseling departments and building principals will need to offer the training, practice, and ongoing support to bring them up to speed. Training is often overlooked and the assumption that counselors, even highly skilled ones, will be ready and set without training can spell an early defeat for the program.

This group leader role is in great contrast to the traditional one-on-one counseling of guidance departments, a service offered behind closed doors with the focus mainly on counselors calling students to their office based on what the counselor and school organization view to be an issue they need help with. It is often a process in which the counselor is in charge of who he counsels or doesn't counsel and what kinds of student problems he deals with or chooses not to.

Who the counselor sees is often based on the needs of the school organization: scheduling students for classes, college admissions, test results, and attendance and discipline issues referred by the assistant principal. This should come as no surprise. Certainly, it's well known to counselors, who have increasingly seen their role become more bureaucratic and administrative-oriented, serving as the go-to person in helping their schools raise academic standards and increase student achievement.

There are tremendous political pressures on school administrators to raise student achievement and they are being forced into enlisting counselors to take a lead role in this effort. Both counselors and administrators are caught up in roles they would rather not have, that is, being survivors rather than doers.

In the author's experience, the inevitable result of this process is that counseling of students for personal problems is given a low priority. Meeting the demands of the school organization always wins out for counselor's time and priority. Therefore, one-on-one counseling as it now exists has limits as a tool to help students resolve their personal issues.

There are many hard-working counselors in our secondary schools who, while they want to help students solve their personal issues, find their job role leaves little time or support to meet this need. Adding an effective group counseling program can be an answer to building a new counseling service to answer the growing needs of students for help with their personal, well-being, and academic needs.

Group counseling programs offer students more involvement in helping solve "their" problems, not the problems the counselor or school organization think they have, but problems they own and are causing them distress. It's a very public offering. An offering in which the group leader is aware his primary role is offering students something "they" see as valuable and able to help them resolve their problems. What he offers is based on a clear understanding of their needs and wants.

It's as if he is creating a menu of possible group choices which students can choose from to help them be more successful, happier, and healthier students. The group counselor can also offer another asset to the guidance and counseling department by expanding his counseling role to include one-on-one personal counseling as well as group counseling, thereby creating a system to move students in and out of each venue depending on their always-changing need and situations.

In closing, there are additional benefits of adding successful group counseling programs. For example, "counseling" will finally be able to take its rightful place as creditable service in the "Guidance and Counseling Departments" of our secondary schools. This service has for too long only been given lip service in the schools' public relation brochures. In fact many students have been left to find help outside the schools or not at all and caring counselors have been frustrated by not being able to help.

Guidance activities and personal counseling for students are both necessary parts of an effective guidance and counseling program. They need to be equal partners and given equal priority and support. Given this teaming of guidance and counseling activities, counselors will finally be able to say both activities can coexist and flourish in their domain; both equal, both valued, and both seen as contributing to the welfare and well-being of students.

1

COUNSELING GROUPS IN SECONDARY SCHOOLS

The Need, Resistance, and Opportunity

Given the huge rise in students entering our secondary schools with emotional, learning, and health and well-being problems, one would think that more guidance and counseling programs would be embracing group work to serve students in need. Sadly this is not the case.

The vast majorities of counselors now serve as quasi-administrators and are primarily involved in the scheduling of students for classes, college admissions and scholarships, mandated testing programs, career and discipline counseling, and data collection for public relation purposes, to demonstrate their school is reaching expectations. The recent books *Wake Up, Counselors: Restoring Counseling Services for Troubled Teens*[1] and *Class Warfare: Focus on "Good" Students Is Ruining Schools*[2] speak directly to the issue that personal counseling for students is given a low priority or not available in many secondary schools.

Add to this scene the reality that more and more guidance programs are losing counselors due to ongoing budget crises, which are more severe in urban and underfunded schools. Given these worsening times, why aren't more guidance programs emphasizing group intervention in order to serve more students rather than only relying on one-on-one interventions?

Group counseling can provide intervention for at-risk students who are desperately in need of relationships with skilled adults who can help them navigate the perils of the life they face each day. Providing once-a-week group counseling for ten to twelve students is not only a time saver for busy counselors, but a positive way to provide support for the many at-risk students not being served.

What issues are standing in the way of counseling programs adopting this valuable and proven strategy? The answer to this question deals with four interrelated issues: organization culture, training, resistance from some administrators and counselors themselves, and the focus on a one-on-one counseling approach rather than utilizing group interventions.

The organizational culture in which secondary school counselors work rarely champions group intervention as a much-needed intervention. Personal counseling is something counselors learn about in graduate school but once inside the school house it is not a skill that is valued or needed, and as a result, it is little used.

The focus of secondary school counselors is on one-on-one meetings with students related to scheduling, college admissions, test evaluations, career counseling, and discipline counseling in which they serve as an auxiliary and support to the school administrators. As a result, most new counselors quickly abandon personal one-on-one and group counseling because they are not required in their role and are little used given the quasi-administrative demand of their job.

What gets quantified gets done. There's often no requirement or expectation to utilize personal counseling interventions. That's only for graduate courses and books about reforming guidance programs. In the real world of school, they exist only for the few counselors who decide on their own to use these interventions to help troubled students. They bravely do so at the risk of being seen and judged as not team members by their quasi-administrator peers.

Being different can be costly to one's job even when one's good intentions are about finding the best way to help at-risk students and acting on it. Group counseling to help troubled students find a new path may be much demanded by students and parents but still not a priority. While there may be much talk in education circles about the need for more group interventions to help students, it usually falls on deaf ears. Secondary school guidance organizations are still operating with a guidance and counseling model developed in the 1950s, a model which has little relevance to today's schools and students.

But organizational culture is not the only culprit. Even if the organizational culture were to change, another major challenge faced by educational reformers set on implementing new intervention programs such as group counseling is that many counselors lack the necessary training to deliver group interventions. While counselors may have had some training on how to lead counseling groups in graduate school, it probably was a very small part of their curriculum and training.

So it should come as no surprise that they arrive as new counselors with little or no real education or training on how to sell, organize, plan, lead, and facilitate helping groups in the school. The energy and idealism they carry over from graduate school to learn more about how to offer personal counseling soon fades as they quickly understand this approach is not a priority. And newly arrived counselors soon find they are working in an organization that provides little of the ongoing training needed to improve their counseling skills and craft.

While there is minimal training for overseeing the mandated testing program, college admissions, scheduling students for classes, and discipline/attendance counseling, training for personal counseling such as group work is left out of the mix. As a result the personal counseling skills of counselors are left unused and dormant.

The supervision they receive involves little focus on their counseling skills and how to improve them. In fact there is often no one on the counseling staff identified and trained to help counselors improve their skills. It's a go-it-alone, learn-how-to-survive environment in many large secondary schools. Improving one's craft as a counselor is pushed aside and learning how to be an efficient quasi-administrator takes over.

Given this organizational culture and lack of training and experience, most counselors aren't going to take the risk to offer group support to students no matter how much they want to help students in need. There are no highlighted signposts with the message "Enter here for training to be a group leader." When some secondary school counselors interested in group work say they are not trained to offer such an intervention, services are right. What they don't say is that there is little expectation in the school organization and culture to use these intervention services. The truth can be risky.

Resistance from counselors themselves and administrators is another culprit. Peer pressure plays an important role in limiting personal counseling in our secondary schools. Counselors with interest in offering helping groups to students are often given strong resistance by veteran counselors who have embraced the quasi-administrative counselor role throughout their careers and have no professional interest in becoming personal counselors either on a one-on-one basis or in group work.

These veteran counselors are often tenured, politically savvy, outspoken, and not about to change their ways, particularly if the administration is satisfied with their role of being a quasi-administrator and serving the growing needs of overwhelmed administrators who are caught up in responding to the neverending mandates from the state and federal level. These administrators themselves are caught in a battle for survival, just like the needy students in their schools.

Given their position of power in the guidance office, these veteran counselors are often quick to remind counselors interested in a personal role, "That's not what we do here. You want to succeed, get tenure? Then give up this idea of doing group work if you want to survive and make it here."

However, as described in chapter 4, there is another compelling reason why more counselors balk at participating in group work in addition to the organizational culture, lack of training, and resistance from other counselors. When counselors rely only on offering one-on-one counseling to students, this intervention goes on behind closed doors. No one other than the counselor and student is able to observe what takes place or assess the counselor's skills or lack of skills.

It's a process carried out in the shadows. As a result, offering one-on-one counseling is often a safe role for counselors. Their skills or lack of skills are not on display as are those of other professionals in the school: teachers, administrators, and coaches. They operate under a cloak of privacy that protects them from the scrutiny faced by their colleagues. This also hinders others from understanding just what counseling is all about and what skills counselors bring to helping students.

But when counselors take on a group leadership role they enter into new territory that is more risky. Risky in the sense that their skills or lack of skills are on full display to every member of the group. The role involves a public performance of how the counselor helps students solve their personal, well-being, and academic problems, a process carried out in full view of group members, not behind closed doors with one student.

Leading groups demystifies the counseling process and brings it out of the shadows for students to see. It allows students to observe the counselor's skills in action and to assess whether he or she has what it takes to help them.

As a result, counselors who choose to stay in a safe, low-risk role usually avoid group work. Counselors who see their role as using groups to help more students are often risk takers interested in learning new skills to expand their mission to help students in need. Those who succeed have the courage, commitment, and political skills to overcome resistance and to persevere. They are the counselors who need to be recruited, supported, and protected when criticism comes their way from peers who become anxious about some counselors upsetting their safe world.

Challenging and changing the organizational culture in secondary schools needs to be a priority of school leaders so group counseling leaders can establish a foothold, train interested counselors in how to organize, plan, lead, and sell a group program, and overcome the resistance that is sure to come their way; resistance which always arrives when new ideas and approaches begin to challenge the existing ways of doing business.

The separation of counselors into two camps, those who see their role as quasi-administrators and those who want their role to include more opportunities for personal counseling, is an outgrowth of the way guidance programs are organized in the school and a major source of resistance to new approaches such as adding group counseling to the services guidance programs provide.

As the second edition of the report "Counseling at the Crossroads"[3] suggests, the role of the counselor is frequently murky, with poorly defined goals that may place them with one foot inside the traditional education system and the other foot in a network of mental and social support services that is not uniformly tied to the rest of the education system, resulting in many counselors reporting a lack of clarity of purpose in both their day-to-day responsibilities and the broader education system.

The path to establishing a group counseling program is like any other school reform. It's one thing to read or discuss it in a graduate class, but when it comes to implementation in the real school world it's no walk in the park. Resistance will be high, resisters will challenge innovation with all the power they have, and their efforts to stop the innovation will not be nice or even professional.

Opponents usually mount a full-fledged attack so they will not be forced to participate in a new program which requires a different way of doing business. To succeed, reforms to help kids in need must find ways to overcome the resistance of naysayers who are quick to unleash a flood of criticism. This is a strategy they know well and that is usually successful, given that there has been very little organizational change in guidance programs since the 1950s.

But needed change may be coming. The "Counseling at the Crossroads" report states the majority of counselors are calling for change in the education system. They report a broken system that does not align with their aspirations for their students. They call for changes in the system, want to help reform efforts, and ask for more support to fulfill their mission.

The American School Counselors Association (ASCA) publication of "The ASCA National Model: A Framework for School Counseling Programs" also supports this call for changes in the way counselors' work is organized.[4] The ASCA model supports the school's overall mission by promoting academic, achievement, career planning, and personal development. The national model consists of four interrelated components: foundation, delivery system, management system, and accountability.

Of special interest to this book is the delivery system, which includes responsive services which address students' direct, immediate concerns as well as counseling, consultation, referral, and system support, which involves training, collaboration, and professional development.

Responsive services include personal one-on-one and group counseling while system supports include the training and professional development needed to update counseling skills that are necessary to help students with academic, personal, social, health, and well-being problems so they can be successful achievers.

Change is difficult, but maybe the "Counseling at the Crossroads" report and the ASCA plan will put pressure on guidance programs to place group counseling as a top priority to help raise student achievement. What we need to be about is making sure that changes in the organizational structure of the school are actually working to respond to students' personal and academic needs and that schools are delivering what has been promised on paper. Promised school reform often becomes watered down and everyone in the school community loses: counselors, administrators, students, parents, and staff.

However there is more to be done in creating an effective group counseling program than simply stating there is a need for group school counseling interventions and providing training for counselors in group work. It's also about how to sell such a program so it is seen as a valuable addition to the counselor's role and not easily derailed by those who will rally against any change in their work schedule and comfort level.

It's about how counseling groups can lead the way in helping large numbers of students resolve their personal problems and take their place in "their" school as successful achievers, no longer sentenced to live out their school lives at the margins: onlookers, and outcast from a school life that can and should be theirs.

KEY IDEAS

- Small group counseling services are an essential component of a comprehensive school counseling program.
- Group counseling is a strategy that allows school counselors to reach more students and maximize their helping role.
- Individual counseling has its limits in that it is often an intervention process that can only reach a small number of students in need. A combination of group counseling and individual counseling works best to create a safety zone for students in need.
- Group counseling services are an effective way of addressing students' academic, well-being, social, and emotional concerns.
- In spite of high student-counselor ratios and increasing demands to take on administrative tasks, the responsibilities of school counselors must evolve to ensure and make accountable an effective way to provide personal counseling to students in order to promote their emotional growth.
- In order to meet this responsibility to deliver effective personal counseling that includes group and individual counseling a new organizational model is now required. This model must allow for the differentiation of staff to include a counselor with the primary role of serving

as a personal counselor and as a trainer for the counseling staff, teachers, administrators, students, support staff, and parents.

- The introduction of this role will help students, staff, administrators, parents, and citizens better understand how counseling interventions work to help students in need and answer the often-raised question, "What do counselors do?"

- Resistance by counselors to taking on a role as a personal counselor to offer group counseling often has its origin in their lack of training and anxiety about moving from their individual counseling role. When counselors say they lack training they are right. Providing the necessary training and support is key to the success of a group counseling program and also to the counselor's own success as a skilled professional. Without the necessary training counselors and their students are both at risk of failure.

- However, where do counselors find the support and training to succeed in offering personal counseling, not simply serving as quasi-administrators to oversee mandated testing programs, college admissions, scheduling students for classes, and discipline/attendance interventions? They need ongoing training opportunities to maintain a high level of counseling skills and be at the top of their counseling game. The lack of opportunities for renewal and new opportunities for career alternatives such as leading counseling groups often leads to settling and becoming resistant to new ideas and change. Education leaders have the responsibility to help their counselors change as times and students need change. Without ongoing training that can be offered by a staff member such as the personal counselor they risk falling into a pattern of doing the minimum, waiting for retirement, and complaining about how their world has changed for the worse and that students and parents no longer appreciate them. Without opportunities for renewal they end up working in a no-risk world where it's more of the same with no challenge. They are allowed to be less than they could have been. This is a recipe for becoming whiners rather than winners, when more training and risk could have produced a better outcome.

- However, as the author suggests, there is a model to follow to make onsite training available for counselors and other staff members. The model is similar to the counseling model for students in which group programs are backed up with an individual counseling component.

The author believes that if students in need of support and help can benefit from this kind of intervention so can staff members such as counselors. In this model the personal counselor is acting as a trainer for his fellow counselors as well as for students, teachers, administrators, support staff, and parents. In this training role the personal counselor is close by, available, and able to utilize both group and individual sessions to hear the concerns of counselors, identify the counseling skills they lack, and help them learn new skills in order to address the changing needs of student, parents, staff, and administrators. He is their mentor and walks the talk with them.

- The author has firsthand experience with a personal counseling role and argues this kind of localized training program can be more effective then returning to graduate school or taking online courses in order to increase counseling skills. Most counselors have a master's degree and some have doctorates. Many are not interested in going back to graduate school to take courses in the late afternoon or evening. Nor are they interested in online courses where there is no human interaction. These venues may not be the best resource for experienced counselors. What they want and need is easy access to training in their own school or district provided by an experienced trainer/mentor who is "one of them" and understands the dynamics, politics, and student, staff, and parent needs in their school.

NOTES

1. William L. Fibkins, *Wake Up, Counselors: Restoring Counseling Services for Troubled Teens* (Lanham, MD: Rowman & Littlefield Education, 2013), 1, 49–54.

2. William L. Fibkins, *Class Warfare: Focus on "Good" Students Is Ruining Schools* (Lanham, MD: Rowman & Littlefield Education, 2013), 76–99.

3. College Board, *Counseling at the Crossroads* (National Office of School Counseling Advocacy, 2011), 6–11, 20, 42.

4. Judy Bowers, Trish Hatch, and American School Counselor Association, *The ASCA National Model: A Framework for School Counseling Programs* (Alexandria, VA: American School Counselor Association, 2005), 1–6.

2

WHY GROUP COUNSELING IS AN IMPORTANT STRATEGY FOR GUIDANCE AND COUNSELING PROGRAMS

Providing a group counseling program for secondary students is a win-win situation for everyone concerned: students, parents, school board members, administrators, counselors, teachers, support staff, concerned citizens, and community health, mental health, law enforcement professionals, and religious leaders.

Group intervention provides financially pressed schools more bang for the buck by providing more counseling services for teens headed for trouble. More students can be seen in groups than in one-on-one counseling, helping them resolve their troubling issues before long-term problems develop.

An active group counseling program, backed up with one-on-one counseling and referrals to community helping agencies, can help ensure a school setting with fewer crises and acting out teens along with the opportunity for troubled teens to become achievers, more socially competent, healthier, and no longer trapped in a cycle of problems, addictions, and failure.

Jacobs, Masson, and Harvill[1] suggest there are many valid reasons to support more groups in the schools. Here are some highlights of their work:

- Groups are an economical and effective way of helping individuals who share similar problems and concerns.

- A school counselor who is responsible for 300 students will barely be able to see each student once during a school year using only a one-on-one format. However, the counselor can meet the needs of many more students by having groups for advising, value clarification, personal growth, support, and problem solving. Having students get together in groups allows them to discover they are not the only ones having particular thoughts, feelings, and concerns.
- Groups can help provide members with a feeling of commonality—we are all in this together—the experience of belonging, the chance to practice new behaviors, the opportunity for feedback, the opportunity for vicarious learning by listening to and observing others, the approximation of real-life encounters, and the pressure to uphold commitments.
- In many instances with teenagers, group counseling is better than individual counseling because teenagers will often talk more readily to each other than to adults.
- Counselors who are effective group leaders have certain characteristics. Admittedly this is a long list and few counselors will possess all the following characteristics. But they represent goals to work toward: excellent listening skills; caring, encouraging, and supporting; clarification and questioning skills; energy; openness; flexibility; warmth; objectivity; trustworthiness; honesty; strength; patience; sensitivity; comfort with oneself and others; liking for people; comfort in a position of authority; confidence in one's ability to lead; and the ability to tune in to other's feelings, reactions, moods, words, and use of eyes and voice.
- In addition, the following skills are important: knowing how to deal with problem situations with members who are excessive talkers, dominators, distracters, resistant, and negative, and who attempt to sabotage what the leader is saying or doing. It is also important to identify allies in the group who can be useful in helping other members, know when the group's work is done and how to close a group, have planning and organizational skills, and understand basic human conflicts and dilemmas.
- Adolescence, ages twelve through nineteen, can be a difficult period in life. Groups can help identify problems, sexual concerns, and difficulties with friends, parents, and school. Groups for preg-

nant teenagers; tobacco, alcohol, and drug users; potential school dropouts; parent divorce and remarriage; sexual, physical, and emotional abuse; stress related to college admissions; and eating disorders can be very helpful to students in need.

- Additional groups for adolescents include self-esteem and self-concept, anger management, living with chemically addicted persons, changing family issues such as separation and divorce, grief and loss, gay and lesbian issues, dating, focus on the future, and entering and returning from residential treatment for tobacco, drug, and alcohol abuse.

- Leading groups with a colleague can be advantageous, especially for the beginner. A major advantage of co-leading is that it is often easier than leading a group alone. A co-leader can provide support and additional ideas for planning, especially when working with intense and difficult groups. Co-leading is also valuable when training an inexperienced person. By co-leading a few times with an experienced leader, a new leader can begin the process of leading on his own and feel reasonably comfortable.

Budd A. Moore's research[2] on the efficacy of group counseling interventions with at-risk adolescents provides a concrete example of many of Jacobs, Masson, and Harvill's observations about groups in secondary schools. Here is a summary of his findings.

The first advantage of using groups with the population in this study is the efficiency of the paradigm. Efficiency has always been a sound rationale for the use of groups in a private practice and in the school setting, where practitioners are being asked to take more and more time away from actual counseling to do many of the more mundane duties required by the modern high school.

Second, bringing together a group of students to explore common concerns is sound justification for group counseling. This researcher believes wholeheartedly in the value of group counseling at the high school level. It offers an excellent forum to discuss common concerns and problems, solve a dilemma, explore feelings and beliefs, and consider a lot of different viewpoints.

It is almost impossible for young people to assess similar information and ways of viewing the world elsewhere. Because of this fact, groups are an efficient vehicle for generating new ideas and solving problems.

The variety of opinions and viewpoints makes the group experience closer to what life is really like. The participants in this study have indeed experienced this.

Third, students often like groups because they make a great contribution to a feeling of commonality among group members. Many times group members discover that they are not alone, that others experience many of the same trials and tribulations of life. One of the first revelations of group participation is that there are others out there who have some of the same concerns as they do.

Developing this togetherness is one of the functions of a group, a commonality that is very reassuring and very therapeutic in its manner to help people cope with the problems that are imposed by modern life. The results of this study clearly demonstrated the effectiveness of group counseling interventions in making a difference along a number of variables related to success in school.

Fourth, group counseling provides a sense of belonging. Human beings have a real and dynamic need to belong. Group members often identify themselves with the group and feel that they are a meaningful part of the whole. This was especially true of the subjects in this study. They liked participating in something where they were not put down and were heard for perhaps for the first time in their lives. Many of the subjects were sad that the groups came to an end at the close of the school.

Fifth, groups provide members with the opportunity to practice new behaviors in an environment that is nurturing and supportive. Subjects were given ample opportunities to examine new behaviors and motivation for behaviors. It was also a place to practice these behaviors with the aim of assisting them to examine and change dysfunctional behaviors that have caused them problems in school. They will probably feel better about using them in the real world.

Sixth, these groups provided the opportunity for members to receive feedback from other members. It is through the expression of this feedback, reactions, and viewpoints that members perhaps begin to think about altering their behavior. That seems to have happened in this study. Group members did think about the subjects we were talking about.

Seventh, the groups afforded members the opportunity to talk about things that mean a great deal to them. They were allowed to compare the important things in their lives with those of other people. Members experienced new realizations through the sympathetic expression of the experiences of others.

Eighth, the groups were a reflection of the society around them. A whole range of everyday emotions was experienced by members of the group.

Last, the group meetings were a place where members made decisions to do different things in their lives. Members declared their intention to change and became aware of ways that they could improve the likelihood of their continuing their education until completion. The groups provided support for making new decisions and also encouraged the members to keep those promises, alter dysfunctional thinking, and change those behaviors that are of importance. All of these universal tenets concerning group counseling were evident in this study with at-risk adolescents.

Here is additional advice for administrators and counselors planning a group counseling program:

- Many adolescent groups work best when they are structured around themes. Themes need to center around the genuine interests of participants.
- The themes that are important to teens are easily accessible to counselors who get out and about in their school and listen to what students have to say as well as interview key members of the teaching staff, administrators, different student groups, support staff, parents, and community health, mental health, and law enforcement professionals. Their feedback can help build a theme-based group counseling curriculum.
- In voluntary groups for teens recruitment is of major importance. Leaders must frame the description and purpose of their groups so they are attractive to students and easily bought into. The words "counseling" and "therapy" should be left out and the emphasis should be on talk and support.
- Personal outreach by the counselor may be required to get group members on board who are resistant to what is seen as "help." Remember teens are often distrusting of professionals who work in offices. Offices often imply to teens that they are in trouble. Teens are more comfortable when invited to talk in their world;

classrooms, hallways, cafeterias, school grounds, dances, sports, activities, libraries, and detention rooms. Holding group counseling sessions in a vacated classroom or conference room often works best.

- Creating school-wide support for a group counseling program means selling it to every student group in the school community. Through this sales campaign students can see the value of such a program and a place for themselves. Students can see if the counselor is someone they can trust, relate to, and open up to, and feel a high degree of safety and comfort around.

- And this selling campaign needs to involve the adults in the school community who work closely with students; administrators, teachers, coaches, club directors, support staff, parents, and community leaders.

Selling a program may be new territory for counselors. Usually counselors use a paper and media trail to inform students of new programs. This may be okay for information on academic programs such as SATs, college application deadlines, and signing up for college visitations. But programs aimed at getting students on board as members of an intervention effort require more than paper and media outreach.

They require a personal effort by the counselor to get out of his office and enter the world of students. It's like a political campaign in which the politician gets out of his office, his safe domain where he calls the shots, and enters the world of the voters. In doing so he shares with them some of his self and how his election will help make their life better.

Same for counselor outreach. He enters the world of his students to tell them why membership in his groups will help make their lives better and resolve some of their pressing issues. He comes not as an all-knowing professional, but as a human being who is interested in his students' well-being and committed to helping them improve their lives.

He walks among each group in the school, interacting with them face to face, ready and set for the give and take that is required in any selling campaign. Teenagers are not won over with brochures and pamphlets. They need to see the person behind the brochures and what he or she can deliver.

Leaders of a group counseling program must be able to pass this test of credibility and not hide in their office using only media outreach to get their troubled student involved. That's a prescription for failure. Students are often blamed for not showing up to programs that would help them by counselors who refuse to sell their wares on the student's turf rather than their own safe turf.

It's like the counselor gave a party and no one came. It is not an uncommon practice for well-intended professionals to blame resistant students for their lack of participation rather than focus on how to change an invitation that fails to resonate with students and falls on deaf ears.

While it is true that possible themes and topics for counseling groups may come from professional articles, journals, and books, the challenge, the necessary hard work, is for group leaders to go out among the students and staff in order to assess the real themes and issues in "their" school and what is relevant to "their" students and "their" lives.

Counselors need to avoid playing it safe, being office-bound, and assuming the suggestions in a professional article about group themes are the only way to go. The key to a group's success lies in counselors finding out what's on the minds and in the hearts and souls of the students who are walking right by him down the school hallways.

Sometimes the hardest lesson for aspiring group counselors to learn is that the role involves aggressive face-to-face recruiting and invitations that get the attention of students who are in need but resistant to being involved in counseling. That's particularly true for both students trapped in failing cycles at the margins of school life and those who are high achievers, trapped in an ongoing cycle of high pressure with little relief.

Here's a description how this aggressive sales pitch plays out with failing students. The same intervention process is also necessary to involve the best and brightest students. Group counselors need to know their students well and deliver an invitation that they can't refuse.

This inviting process often works well because students in need are not accustomed to counselors entering their world and singling them out to be participants. For many students this kind of invitation is a compliment and affirmation that they are valued for who they are, not their academic record. Being wanted for who they are, not what they know or don't know, is a feeling many students in need have never experienced.

As suggested in *Wake Up, Counselors: Restoring Counseling Service for Troubled Teens*,[3] students involved in a failure cycle often resist initial overtures by counselors to help them and involve them in one-on-one and group counseling. Often these students are distrustful of being "helped," seeing it as an effort by school authorities to straighten them out and change their ways.

In these cases, it is easier for students to connect with life on the margins, where there is an acceptance of the behaviors the school cannot condone. Well-trained and experienced counselors welcome this challenge and are aggressive in visiting where students hang out and initiating a dialogue with students, getting to know them, and using their persuasive skills to connect these students to a counseling process.

As Robert L. Sinclair and Ward J. Ghory suggest, forward-looking school principals, counselors, teachers, and parents bend over backward to create positive ties for positive connections.[4] Students who are becoming marginalized receive a good deal of attention. Understanding how and why students become marginalized becomes a basis for action.

Therefore, the work of understanding how and why students become marginalized involves counselors collecting data by fully participating in the daily lives of marginalized students, whether it be in the counseling office, the classroom, the hallways, or the cafeteria, before or after school activities, or at home and in community life. That means they go where the action is and understand how these students interact in their world, hearing their language and learning firsthand what is going on in their lives.

Through this investigative process, counselors develop a more adequate picture of the issues preventing marginalized students from becoming achievers, and as a result they are able to develop an intervention plan that fits each student. Students respond to help when the message seems to fit them and their needs and is delivered by a counselor who knows them well and has established a degree of credibility, not a counselor who is office-bound and only sees a student for scheduling, disciplining, and subtle warnings to shape up or be gone.

Sinclair and Ghory remind us that it is sobering to realize that any student is at risk of becoming at least temporarily disconnected from full and productive involvement in classrooms and school. They can be quickly knocked out of a pattern of productivity and go unnoticed in school for long periods, particularly in our large secondary schools with populations of over 2,000 students.

Unfortunately, these problems do not go away. They fester and can reach a critical point in the late teen years. And as a result of a lack of needed intervention, problems over time often become more complicated and serious. It is important for the "go to" personal counselors in the school to identify problematic students early and intervene. Time is not always a healer.

In this role, the counselor is not only an aggressive helper willing to seek out marginal students in their own haunts and comfort zones, but he also serves as a sort of investigative reporter who asks himself the following questions about the student in need of help.

- What gives here? Why is this student unable and/or uninterested in achieving?
- What habits has he developed that are preventing his return to the mainstream of school life?
- What kind of interventions might help this student?

As these questions begin to be answered, the counselor's next step is to document this data for himself as well as for the building principal at the once-a-week principal-counselor meetings. In this way, the story of the student in question becomes known to the principal, and the student is no longer simply a number identified only as a member of the at-risk group but is a real kid worth paying attention to and helping.

Counseling marginalized students is a two-way process. For the counselor it's finding the right tone, the right style, the right time to connect with a student and sell him or her the idea that the counselors have something of value to offer, demonstrating that he cares and offers support, comfort, trust, and, when needed, helpful confrontation. For the student it means the opportunity to find a caring adult who knows something about her world and who might be able to help.

It means finding a safe place, a cocoon, in which she can tell her story no matter how difficult this story may be, and she can somehow begin to have some aspirations, hopes, and excitement about turning her life around. This kind of help can often go on outside the counselor's office with lunch in the cafeteria, walks around the school track, and even while playing basketball in the gym.

Troubled students usually avoid the offices in their school for good reason. For them being summoned to an office, even a counselor's office, often sends the message that they are in trouble. A veteran high school personal counselor told me that he often held counseling sessions in the back of the school where the smokers hung out. Troubled kids have their safe places and counselors need to know where they are and use them.

Help can go on in many places. It usually works best where students are comfortable. As such, personal counselors need to pay attention to their own office environment and make them welcoming settings, not just an office that is designed to "do business" and then get the students out, or use attractive spaces in the school.

Personal counselors are different from counselors who interact with students around clerical tasks such as class scheduling, testing, etc. The world of personal counselors is all about finding meaning in encounters and situations with students and asking such questions as: What is this student's school and home life like? What goes on for him in school and at home? Is he a loner or connected to some group in the school or community? How does he see himself? Does he have dreams, hopes, and aspirations? What has gone wrong in his life to separate him from the mainstream of school life?

In this role, the counselor participates in the lives of students and tries to overcome their resistance by respecting the student's norms, values, conflicts, and pressures although they may be very different from those of the counselor's own life. Acceptance of the other is critical for the offer of help to be welcomed. As the counselor gains entrance into the real lives of students, he often finds this territory very unfamiliar compared to his own present-day life.

The world that students inhabit may seem problematic and to some extent unnatural to the counselor. As he gets to know a student, he may find himself learning lessons he didn't foresee. Helping students from diverse backgrounds can unsettle even an experienced counselor. Counselors are warned in their training that they may become involved with students who have problems that can unnerve them, make them feel anxious, and make them want to flee.

Counselors who choose the quasi-administrative role often do so in order to avoid involvement in real-life stories of students who have seen many tragedies in their lives and seem lost, unable to find their place. Skilled personal counselors are not immune to the pain of their students but are committed to staying with them as a helping process evolves, not an easy task or a role for the faint of heart. When counselors enter the real world of students and observe them in their own environment and culture, they often learn answers to questions that the counselors would not have had the sense to ask.

This kind of intervention can be risky and out of what is seen as the "normal" work that counselors perform, but in the author's experience it is a proven way to get students interested, motivated, and on board the helping process that groups can offer. This process is also backed up by easily available one-on-one counseling. What we are talking about is similar to what retailers do to find out what their customers' needs are. They do the necessary research and hold focus groups to learn what motivates the buyer to come in the door or go online to shop.

Successful group counselors follow the same script. They go out and ask students what is on their minds and what their issues are, and demonstrate how the counselors can help them by inviting them to join a group that can meet their needs. A counselor probably doesn't call his outreach research or a focus group process but in fact he is, like the retailers, assessing what his customers, the students, need to open the door to help and walk in.

In a real sense this outreach helps him build a group counseling program that is student-based rather than his own idea of what he thinks they may need. It's their program, their curriculum for help. He is simply the facilitator who orchestrates the process. His skill is in making their issues and cries for help be heard and responded to.

KEY IDEAS

- Effective counseling groups are student-driven. The curriculum for group work is built on the needs of students, not the school, parents, or community.
- Counseling groups offer students a source of support that is similar to what a healthy and caring family lifestyle can offer. This lifestyle is

often missing in their lives. For example, groups can provide a feeling of togetherness, belonging, hope for the future, a place to heal their wounds when failures visit their lives, and a way to learn how to go on.

- A counselor who lead groups often has a positive history with students. Students see him as the person to go to when trouble visits them. He is a wise adult figure who seems to have the special gifts and skills to comfort, sometimes confront, and help them learn how to turn their lives around no matter how painful their lives have become. It's as if he has walked in their shoes in his own life, and perhaps he has. He intuitively knows things about how hard life can be such as on a new student's first day in school, when a parent suddenly dies, the anger and sadness a student feels due to the divorce of her parents, the isolation faced by a newly pregnant student, and the shame felt by a student whose father was arrested for drunk driving and is a page-one story in the local paper. He is a mentor who they can begin to model their life after.

- However, the personal counselor needs to walk a fine political line to be successful. He needs to avoid coming off as a savior or messiah, or appearing to be a buddy and friend with students. These kinds of behaviors may not sit well with his fellow counselors, teachers, and administrators who see him as a rising star, a lone ranger only interested in his career, not a team player committed to the overall success of the guidance program and the school. This kind of criticism goes with the territory. Educators are often sensitive to the success of peers and tend to view them as only interested in promoting themselves. For example, change, new ways of offering counseling services such as group counseling, can belittle the lifetime achievements of quasi-administrator counselors who now feel less valued and fear the loss of the positive regard they once enjoyed. Jealousy of another's success is not uncommon in organizational life, including schools.

- Therefore the personal counselor needs to be humble and accepting of his peers even though they may not agree with or support his view of counseling. His gift to help kids in need may appear to be grandstanding and causing a negative light to shine on counselors and staff who are not personal counseling and student oriented and feel disrespected. The most important goal for him is to avoid making enemies in the guidance department, staff, and administration who may interfere with his counseling work. Being quiet about his successes and being a team player helps to keep his critics at bay.

NOTES

1. Ed E. Jacobs, Robert L. Masson, and Riley L. Harvill, *Group Counseling Strategies and Skills* (Pacific Grove, CA: Brooks/Cole, 2002), 2, 19, 25, 119.

2. Budd A. Moore, "The Efficacy of Group Counseling Interventions Employing Short-Term Rational Emotive Behavior Therapy in Altering Beliefs and Behaviors of At-Risk Adolescents" (dissertation, Virginia Polytechnic Institute, Blacksburg, VA, 1999), 139–41.

3. William L. Fibkins, *Wake Up, Counselors: Restoring Counseling Services for Troubled Teens* (Lanham, MD: Rowman & Littlefield Education, 2013), 1, 49–54.

4. Robert L. Sinclair and Ward J. Ghory, "Last Thing First: Realizing Equity by Improving Conditions for Marginal Students," in *Access to Knowledge: An Agenda for the Nation's Schools*, ed. John Goodlad and Pamela Keating (New York: College Entrance Examination Board, 1990), 67–69.

3

WHAT DOES A MODEL GROUP COUNSELING PROGRAM LOOK LIKE?

Educators planning a group counseling program need to begin their planning with a vision of how to implement and sustain the program. Each school presents its own set of dynamics, student needs, and areas of resistance to change and new programs. "One size, one vision" does not fit every school. Here is the author's prescription of how a clear vision and early planning involving many sectors of the school and community can result in a successful program with many open doors of help for students.

As the author suggests in "How to Start a School Group Counseling Program,"[1] there are three early planning steps required to build a successful group counseling program. First, the implementation process calls for gaining support from the entire school community: administrators, staff, students, support staff, and professionals involved in community health, mental health, and law enforcement.

Second, the program needs to be composed of a number of different counseling groups that will be able to respond to the personal, academic, and well-being needs of every student group in the school, not just the acting-out, so-called troublemakers.

Third, the project requires the establishment of a network of helping professionals in the school and community who are positioned to identify, engage, and refer kids in need to the program. These professionals work on the frontlines of the school and community. They are the eyes and ears that can easily detect the warning signs of students headed for trouble.

In regard to the first step, gaining support from the entire school community, each group needs to be informed as to why group counseling is now needed, how the program can help students resolve problems and become healthy, secure, and better achievers, how they can support and refer students to the group program, and how they can provide the political backing much needed when new programs are in the first stage of implementation.

In-person outreach by key administrators and counselors involved in the project is critical. A human face must be put on the project and lines of communication clearly spelled out. As in all new projects, there will be resistance and mistakes will be made. Having the support of key administrators, staff, students, parents, and community leaders can serve to fend off critics and prevent halting the project before it establishes a welcome presence in the school and community.

The second step, creating a number of different groups to meet the personal, academic, and well-being needs of students from every group in the school, calls for reminding members of the school and community that each student in the school can find themselves at risk in their school career and need the intervention of either one-on-one or group counseling or both. Many teenagers experience problematic issues in the course of their high school career. It's a normal process, not to be afraid of, but rather confronted in the school culture.

Acting out goes with the territory of being a teenager, no matter how problem-free their community appears to be on the surface. However, sometimes teens who have high-achieving parents with over-the-top expectations for their children are more at risk than their less successful peers. They tend to not act out in school and cause trouble. Therefore it is often difficult for them to seek help, as they are viewed as teens having it all with no problems.

Even in today's positive view of counseling, seeking help is often viewed as a weakness by the parents of the best and brightest students and the students themselves. Many see the process of getting help as a crack in their veneer of greatness. Successful students and parents who appear to live problem-free lives may be hiding troubles behind their seemingly perfect public persona.

As a result the leader of a proposed group counseling program needs to stress that the group counseling program will focus on serving the needs of every student, not just the students who cause trouble, act out, have failing grades, and show little interest in school or higher education. Student problems are not owned by marginal students. Every student can be at risk no matter how strong and well they appear. The bottom can unexpectedly fall out in their lives and bad things can happen to good kids.

For example, the best and brightest students are often at risk for abusing prescription stimulants such as "good grade pills" prior to exams and tobacco, alcohol, and other drugs on weekends as a way to relieve this pressure. In a sense they can be more at risk than their presumably high-risk peers and it requires a great deal of trust building to get them involved in a helping group and one-on-one counseling for their parents. The mantra of the group counseling program needs to be "hiding problems is not OK, having problems and seeking help is OK."

However, group leaders need to be cautioned not to allow the groups to be used by students as a way to bash the school administration and policies. In the author's experience some students may target the administrators as bad guys and ride that theme as a way to hide and avoid addressing their own problems caused by outside-of-school forces such as sexual, emotional, and physical abuse, family breakup, family addictions, absent parents who committed more to their job than family, and living an impoverished life.

While school administrators can be lightning rods for student anger and not perfect, group members shouldn't be allowed to take over the group and blame them for all the wrongs in the students' world. The personal counselors must be adept at not letting the group sessions be used only as a forum to bash administrators and avoid the real purpose of the group which is to identify and address their own issues. Student anger toward administrators is part of the culture of secondary schools, but it should not become the sole purpose of the group.

The third step requires a plan to utilize the helping skills and resources of many caring school staff, students, parents, and community health, mental health, and law enforcement professionals for referral to the group counseling project. These groups are on the frontlines of the school and community and are ideally positioned to observe students headed for trouble, engage them, and help direct, assist, and help them.

As the saying suggests, "it takes a village to raise a child." It also "takes a village" to counsel a troubled child and help make him or her well. While the leader of a group counseling program may be a full-time counselor, he will need the support and skills of many dedicated members of the school community to help make the program successful. Here is an example of the team members needed to serve as an integral part and back-up of a group counseling project:

- *School Nurse.* The school nurse comes in daily contact with at-risk students. She understands that many at-risk students have multiple problems. For example, they may be addicted to alcohol, another drug, or tobacco. They may have an eating disorder. They may live in an abusive situation. Many school nurses have an attractive, safe, and easily accessible helping environment. She can be an effective liaison between the troubled student, the school staff, the parents, or community agencies. Many troubled students avoid the anonymity of a physician's office in favor of this familiar and trusted professional.

- *Caring Teachers.* Not all teachers are natural helpers, but many are. Teachers are naturally positioned to observe the first signs of trouble: a bruised face, chronic absences, tardiness, inability to concentrate, solitariness, and self-imposed isolation. Students in trouble will often let a favorite teacher know that they need help. They can intervene with simple words of concern, "How are you doing" or "Let's talk," and when needed, referral to the right school or community resource for further help.

- *Coaches and Physical Education Teachers.* Coaches will notice changes in the performance of student athletes that often signal personal problems. Physical education teachers may notice problems with students as well. Signs of abuse, depression, and isolation from other students can show up and are easily noticed in play activities. For example, the student who does not get dressed for gym or refuses to attend class may be covering up physical or emotional abuse by an abusive parent. These professionals, armed with reliable referral sources, can sound the alarm, share their concerns, and open up a lifeline for support before the problems get worse and a crisis occurs.

- *Club and Extracurricular Mentors.* Theater directors, chess club directors, band and choral directors, and others are involved with creative students, often "the best and brightest," who are not thought of as at-risk. However, these high-achieving students sometimes tire of their role as standard-bearers for the school and look for ways out. As high achievers, they are not used to asking for help. Club directors and members are in a good position to pick up their distress signals. The theater director may notice that her lead actor is suddenly blowing his lines. An expression of concern may lead to a deeper conversation and appropriate action.

- *Support Staff.* In many schools, the secretary in the dean's office interacts with troubled students all day and often becomes a trusted confidante. Helping conversations are often at the core of these relations. For example, "Frank, please get some help with your smoking problem. Listen to your cough. Go talk to Dr. Fibkins, he has a smoking cessation program. If you want I'll call him and set up an appointment, please do it." Or the schoolyard monitor who observes students cutting classes and smoking may also be someone the students trust. Support staff are an underrated but powerful source of intervention and referral.

- *Parents.* Many parents are natural helpers. They have raised teenagers and they know what works and what doesn't. They have been through the angst of adolescence. They know who is headed for trouble in their neighborhoods. If encouraged, they can play a useful role in your school. Just like others on this list, they can express concern and make referrals to appropriate school and community resources such the personal counselor, serve as a source of support as the intervention process proceeds, and act as a parent/family surrogate for kids in need so they feel safe and belong.

- *Community Mentors.* In a competent community, skilled adults serve as mentors and caretakers for troubled teens. Many schools are realistic about the limits of their helping recourses and cultivate relationships with law enforcement, recreation, medical, social service, and mental health professionals. Building these links is a way to extend the safety net beyond the school day.

- *Administrators.* Surprisingly, many administrators do not see themselves as a source of help to troubled students. They may think that they are not trained to be helpers or that their role has only to do with curriculum or discipline. However, many administrators need to be reminded of their intimate role with students and not underestimate their skills and ability to help students. Every day they come in direct contact with students who are acting out, addicted, suicidal, or headed into the criminal justice system. Their intervention and referral can save lives. They can share their concern, encourage the student to tell his or her story, listen, empathize, and direct them to reliable sources of help such as the personal counselor. These are simple steps that can serve to model a positive helping role for staff, students, and parents and expect them to do the same, becoming helpers rather than observers and adding a new dimension to their administrative role.

There are many staff members and community professionals looking to add new vitality and interest to their career by serving in a helping and referral role for students in need.

However, a planned group counseling program needs more than a vision that fits the needs of their school and students. First-hand information and models of successful group counseling programs are needed to guide program leaders on how to proceed. Experience counts, the good and bad news, when new programs are being planned in the school setting. Here is an example of a model of how to start a group counseling program developed by the author and his support team at Shoreham-Wading River High School in suburban Long Island, New York.

The support team was made up of the high school principal, school nurse, school psychologist, faculty members, coaches, parents, and community professionals. This was a diverse group who had positive connections with a variety of student groups and could target the growing number of students with personal, academic, and well-being problems. The model presented here involves four critical steps:

1. An example of the talking points educators can use to sell and promote the program.

2. A description, or case study, of the implementation process and what was learned.
3. The mandatory counseling group: an example presented to highlight how counseling groups help students, parents, and the school organization.
4. A description, or case study, of the mandatory counseling group and what was learned, its value to the school, students, and parents.

The rationale, the selling point, for convincing educators, students, parents, and community members needs to be straightforward, convincing, easily understood, and supported. Here's the kind of dialogue, or talking points, needed to sell the school community on this program.

TALKING POINTS FOR GROUP COUNSELING PROGRAM

Talk with students from high schools throughout the country on any given day and you quickly learn that students are dealing with tremendous pressures. They are pressured to appear older, have early sexual experiences, spend money and acquire things, be their own nurturers (mom and dad both work), and have the SAT scores, class rank, grades, wardrobe, hairstyle, family, and weight needed to fit in with their peers.

Often they are pressured by peers to find relief in alcohol, tobacco, and other drugs. And, if that's not enough, when they fail to realize their academic and personal dreams, many of these students have no one to confide in, no place to go, to learn how to handle the pressures of living in 2014.

In communities across America, many parents are working two jobs to survive in a tough economy. At the same time, recreation and youth agencies are being forced to cut back on personnel and school districts are eliminating teaching and counseling positions to adhere to austerity budgets, often the younger staff members who relate well to students.

The result is that just when the need for help is greater than ever, school guidance and counseling departments must answer the question, "What can be done to provide counseling for students who bring family troubles, abuse, tobacco, alcohol and drug addictions, and sexuality issues to school in this time of limited resources?"

Clearly, limited resources are here to stay. Schools must use the counseling resources already in place to develop programs that reach and help the largest number of students. A strong group counseling program can serve this purpose and at the same time be a means to empower and train students to take a leadership role in helping their peers. Here's a model:

CASE STUDY OF THE IMPLEMENTATION PROCESS AND WHAT WAS LEARNED

The group counseling program began the summer before school opened in September when the school counselor who was to lead the program attended a training program at the Hazelden Institute in Centre City, Minnesota. Hazelden Institute is world-famous, offering rehabilitation for drug, tobacco, and alcohol addiction and training programs for professionals in education, medicine, psychology, religion, and social service. The focus of the training was on how to provide one-on-one and group counseling to help students troubled by personal, academic, and well-being problems such as drug, tobacco, and alcohol addictions.

Upon his return the counselor met with his support team to share how his training could be used in the forthcoming group counseling program. Sharing information, getting every team member involved and on the same page, was the first goal of the program. Beginning with the first day of school, he set out to assess the needs and concerns of students through conversations during individual counseling, attending school dances and athletic events, and visiting student hangouts in the cafeteria and detention room. He met with tobacco smokers who gathered off school grounds, and visited with students at off-campus sites such as McDonalds, Burger King, and the local pizza parlor.

There was no time to lose given the waiting needs of students. In these meetings many students expressed concerns about pressures from college admissions; poor school performance; drug, tobacco, and alcohol use and abuse; health problems such as obesity, bulimia, and anorexia; abusive relationships with boy/girlfriends, peers, family members; and poor relationships with peers, teachers, and parents.

In addition to talking with students, the counselors talked with administrators, teachers, support staff, coaches, and parents about their views of students' concerns and which students might benefit from group participation. By November of that year, the kinds of groups that were needed became apparent and groups were organized so that students could share their concerns and find solutions. The support team decided the group would have a maximum of ten students, meet for one class period per week, and offer ten to twelve sessions. Groups that were started included:

- *Five-Hours-a-Day Smoking Cessation Groups.* Three groups with ten students each were offered to help students who wanted to minimize or refrain from smoking. Students and leaders followed a self-help curriculum designed by them, and the school nurse acted as a co-facilitator.
- *Forty-Eight-Hour Group.* Through previous discussions with students, the facilitator knew that many students were sober during the school week, but used drugs, tobacco, and alcohol on weekends. Failing in past attempts to cut back or stop using alone, they wanted to learn refusal skills beyond just saying no. The forty-eight-hour group was formed to meet this need.
- *College Admissions Group.* Students in grades eleven and twelve often need to share their concerns and to learn how to handle the pressures of wanting to get into "the college of their choice." Themes discussed in these groups included high expectations by parents, teachers, and counselors, peer competition, concern over SAT scores, over-involvement in activities to enhance school records, and dealing with rejections. These groups were particularly helpful to gifted students experiencing a great deal of pressure throughout the admission process.
- *Alternative High School Group.* Two groups were developed to provide ongoing support for students in the alternative program at the school. Twenty-three students were in the program, and eighteen participated in two ongoing groups dealing with building self-esteem, improving school performance, developing hopes and dreams, and handling difficult school and family situations.
- *Returning from Rehab Group.* Students who were returning to school from rehabilitation for drug- and alcohol-related problems received both group and one-on-one counseling support. Many of

these students were counseled into rehabilitation programs by the counselor and now needed re-entry support.

- *Mandatory Counseling Group.* This group provided ongoing support for students who had been using drugs and alcohol at school activities, mainly at school dances. School policy required all impaired students to be assessed by the counselor. The group was established to provide long-term support following assessment.
- *Grade Level Groups.* These groups were designed to help students deal with the particular problems that arise in grades nine, ten, eleven, and twelve.

Counseling groups became the backbone of the Student Assistance Program (SAP) at Shoreham-Wading River High School. About 150 students, 25 percent of the total school population, were helped. The counselor devoted at least 2.5 days to group work and the remaining time to individual counseling and training staff as advisors and students as helpers.

Many students, who otherwise would have had to wait for individual counseling appointments, received help through group participation. Counseling groups provide more bucks for the dollar and increase the opportunities for more students to resolve their problems before they become major issues. The program also offered the counselor the opportunity to train and encourage students to informally help their peers, electing to make a commitment to watch out and care for them and lead them to sources of help.

It is important to understand that developing and maintaining an effective group counseling program requires careful planning, excellent group facilitating skills, a strong relationship with students, and the support and trust of school administrators, teachers, support staff, and parents. But it also requires attention to all the minute details needed.

For example, the role of the counselor leading the group counseling program encompasses aspects ranging from making sure group members receive passes from classes in order to participate to ameliorating conflicts with teachers who resist releasing students to attend groups, supporting students when a beloved teacher dies suddenly, and teaching students to support a peer who has attempted suicide. Minding the store, keeping things simple, and having a good sense of school politics and school climate/culture are critical.

The counselor also needs to develop a privacy shield in order to maintain the confidentiality and privacy of each student, helping programs die quickly when the word spreads among students that their dirty laundry has become a topic of conversation in the faculty room or at the teachers' happy hour after school on Friday.

AN EXAMPLE OF THE GROUPS OFFERED— THE MANDATORY COUNSELING GROUP

A valuable lesson learned in this project was the use of tough love to help students on the way to addictions. Membership in all of the previously identified groups was voluntary, open to any students with the specific need for such a group, except the mandatory counseling groups. There are times when encouraging students to volunteer for group membership is not enough. Tough love is needed. For example, students who are addicted or on the road to addiction and bringing their problems to the school campus needed quick interventions.

When students act out, ignore the rules of the school community, and abuse alcohol and drugs at school functions, they need to be sent a clear message that this kind of behavior will not be tolerated. There are consequences for their behavior, but help is close by. In most cases suspensions from school do little to help these students. Putting them back on the streets often leads to more addiction.

One of the lessons learned in this project was that required participation in the mandatory counseling group proved to be an effective way for addicted students or those on the way to addiction to be helped and, if needed, referred to community health and mental health professionals or rehabilitation.

IMPLEMENTATION OF THE MANDATORY COUNSELING GROUP AND WHAT WAS LEARNED

Here is a description of how the author used his student assistance counseling role to enhance the group counseling program and bring needed help to acting-out addicted students who were involved in ongoing suspension and headed for dropping out unless help was on the way. The title of the author's article is "Teens + School + Alcohol = Mandatory Counseling."[2] Here's the story.

High school administrators and other staff across the country are increasingly concerned with students who use alcohol and drugs at school functions. In fact, many schools have instituted strict policies that require automatic suspension for students found to be impaired at school dances, pep rallies, and other school activities.

Sending a strong message to students that the school will not tolerate the use of alcohol on school grounds is an important first step. Unfortunately, many schools stop their intervention after the student is caught, the parents are informed, and the student is suspended.

The student then returns to school only to find him or herself the center of gossip, rumors, and ridicule. Often, no ongoing counseling is made available to help the student, who by this time feels guilty and embarrassed by his or her acting-out drinking/drugging behavior. Some of these students are addicted and need further intervention. Abusing alcohol/drugs in a very public way, such as falling down at a homecoming dance, is a cry for help. "Look at me—I need help" is often the message being sent.

Many students caught using alcohol/drugs may not be addicted, but they need intervention to help them deal effectively with the episode and the issues they will face as they re-enter school after suspension. These students need ongoing counseling and support in learning more about their own needs and why they chose alcohol/drugs for relief. They also need to learn how to relate to peers, parents, and teachers who may see them as a problem rather than an adolescent who needs help and support.

The student can use this episode as an opportunity for change if the school creates the right conditions for help. What are the right conditions for change and how can they be implemented in the schools? Given the implementation of the group counseling at Shoreham-Wading River High School the conditions were right for its students. Those students caught drinking/drugging at school activities could be helped with mandatory counseling. Being required to attend the mandatory counseling group might be considered a lucky break. At least they had been given the opportunity for help while their heavy drinking/drugging peers secretly continued on the road to addiction.

The high school was one of a few in the area that still held many dances for students. Many neighboring schools had eliminated or reduced the number of dances because of problems with alcohol and drug abuse. Administrators and staff at Shoreham-Wading River High School didn't want to penalize the entire student body by eliminating or reducing the number of dances, but were concerned about how to help impaired students. They knew that suspensions didn't really help students to resolve their problems with alcohol.

As a result the school administration, SAP counselor, and his team decided to make counseling mandatory for students determined to be impaired at school functions. Ninety-five percent of the referrals for mandatory counseling came from students impaired at school dances and pep rallies. The SAP counselor became involved with the students on the Monday morning following the incident.

The assistant principal notified him of the student's name and informed the student to set up an appointment with the counselor within three days because the school would be buzzing with rumors and the student would need support. Because the counselor had worked as a counselor in the middle school with many of the students, he had no difficulty making contact with them. In most cases, they wanted help.

Lessons Learned from This Intervention

Through counseling thirty-one students, the SAP counselor learned the following:

- Students from all grade levels used alcohol/drugs at school dances, with students in grade eleven using alcohol most often.
- The gender breakdown was about equal for males and females, seventeen males and fourteen females.
- The reasons students gave for using alcohol/drugs at school dances included:

  - Need for relief from pressures of adolescent life.
  - Concern over grades, college relationships, failed dreams, and appearance, usually with females related to weight and feeling "too fat."

- Their reactions to being caught were:

  - Why did I do this to myself and my family? I should have seen it coming. I didn't set out to do this, it just happened.
  - The teachers and other kids all know; I'm so embarrassed. I'll never get over this. Everyone is looking at me when I walk down the hall.
  - I'm not like this; I'm not an alcoholic.

More than 40 percent of the impaired students continued in individual and group counseling after the required assessment. Students who became impaired at school dances and other activities usually had other troubles. They needed help, and they usually responded to counseling if the process was offered as one of support rather than a reprimand or penalty.

Testifying to the success of the program, not one of these thirty-one students seen in the counseling group had a repeat offense. Some of them became peer leaders in a forty-eight-hour program to help other students get through the weekend without drinking. One student entered a thirty-day rehab. Upon returning to school she became a model student. Her story will be featured in a forthcoming book by the author entitled *No Easy Way Out*.

HOW THE RESULTS OF A GROUP COUNSELING PROGRAM CAN CREATE MORE OPEN DOORS FOR HELP

Once educators, students, and parents become involved in observing the positive aspects of the helping process such as the group counseling program, they are often on the lookout for opportunities to be helpers themselves. Leaders of successful group counseling programs are ideally positioned to train these potential caregivers in the helping process and use their skills to expand the schools' helping network.

The case of members of the mandatory group counseling program taking on the role of helping students in the forty-eight-hour group to reduce or stop their drinking/drugging on weekends is a useful example of students who are helped being called upon to help their peers.

Here are some other examples. Create opportunities for students to serve as peer helpers, for teachers to serve as advisors, for parents to serve as sources of support for other parents and kids, and for administrators to see their role as a helper for every member of the school community. A school community in which all members can become their brother's keeper, not look the other way when they observe students, teachers, support staff, parents, or administrators heading toward the margins of school and community life, fosters the understanding that someday these members may be in the same place and need help as well.

KEY IDEAS

- The main focus on building a group counseling program is to make sure it is localized and home-grown, and that it addresses the problems and issues of students in "their" school, rather than being a model borrowed from another school where the dynamics, setting, culture, and student issues are very different. Many group counseling programs fail because counselors replicate a program taken from a professional article or book, rather than taking the time and effort to reach out to their students, find out what their needs are, and identify what it takes to get them involved. Invite/empower them to help build a program that is "theirs."
- The localized, home-grown process also needs to include a support team made up of key members of the school community and community advocates who work closely with students and are aware of their needs and issues. The personal counselor, the facilitator for the group counseling program, must be careful to not go it alone in building the program. He needs a back-up team who enjoy positions of power and respect in the school and community in order for the program to be seen as needed and legitimate as well as being positioned to make referrals to the program.
- While the main focus of building the group counseling program is on listening to the needs and issues of students, the school organization also has needs and is a big player in its success. What schools need is not at odds with what their students need. Schools want programs that can help their students resolve their academic, well-being, and

personal problems so they can become better achievers and good citizens. And so do the majority of students who come to school each day. The personal counselor must be adept at not allowing the school organization to be targeted as the only bad guy in town and held responsible for all the problems affecting students involved in the group program. While schools do play a role as an authority figure and are not perfect institutions, the majority of educators do their best, although they are human and imperfect. The personal counselor must be careful to not let the group members spend all their time bashing the school organization rather than addressing the other, often hidden, problems affecting their lives.

NOTES

1. William L. Fibkins, "How to Start a Group Counseling Program," *Student Assistance Journal* (September/October 1994): 26–28.

2. William L. Fibkins, "Teens + School + Alcohol = Mandatory Counseling," *Student Assistance Journal* (March/April 1995): 32–33.

4

THE FIRST STEP IN READYING COUNSELORS AS GROUP LEADERS

Listening to Their Concerns

The following queries are culled from the author's training program to ready school counselors to be group leaders. In these training sessions the author has found that while many counselors are trained in individual counseling, a surprising few have experience in group leadership.

As a result, in most secondary schools counselors use individual counseling as the primary mode of intervention. Counselors get comfortable working with one student at a time. It's the way it's done. And the majority of these one-on-one sessions are for scheduling for classes, test results, college admissions, and attendance and discipline counseling. Appointments for personal counseling pale in comparison to other student outreach by counselors.

The counseling process as it is now carried out in our secondary schools provides a safe environment for counselors. The counselor is in charge and controls the focus and tempo of the interviews. There is little risk for him or her and not much is known about what goes on behind the counselor's closed doors. Unlike other professionals in the school—teachers, administrators, or coaches—the counselor's skills or lack of skills are not on display for others to see. The counseling process is cloaked in privacy, carried on behind closed doors, and holds a shadowy place in schools where most student-staff interactions are very public.

When critics ask "What do counselors do?" the usual response is a presentation about how counselors help students get into college, achieve high grades, get higher test scores, increase attendance, and reduce the dropout rate. There is seldom any data about how the counseling process works to help students with their personal and well-being problems or about the skills required by counselors to know their students well and connect with their lives.

While there is much discussion in schools about what teaching styles and interventions work best to increase student achievement, there is little discussion about which counseling styles and interventions work best to help students solve their problems and become better achievers. What gets measured gets done and what is measured for counselors is data about college admissions, test scores, scheduling students for classes, attendance, and lowering discipline and dropout rates.

These are top-priority tasks for secondary counselors. Counseling students to solve academic, personal, and well-being problems is not a top priority for counselors. However, it is often given a top rating in school districts' public relation releases which highlight counseling intervention to not let one student fall between the cracks.

Adding a group counseling outreach lead by well-trained, committed, and courageous counselors is an important step in demystifying the counseling process and demonstrating that the guidance and counseling department is not leaving students in need to fend for themselves or to find resources outside the school community for help.

However, it makes no sense to force counselors who have no interest or skills to lead groups. What is required is knowing each counselor well, recognizing their gifts and skills to counsel students in need, encouraging them to get on board as group leaders, and making sure they are well trained, supported, and affirmed for their interventions.

Groups are more complex than individual counseling. Counselors who lead groups are now dealing with a large number of students, many of whom are often plagued by more than one problem. While many students say they have joined the group to get help, they arrive hesitant to risk disclosure. Getting students to talk and be open in individual counseling can be difficult even for well-trained counselors, but in groups that challenge is magnified.

Dealing with eight to ten students can be risky for counselors. They don't have the control they think they have in individual counseling sessions. Nor do they have the protective shield in groups that they have in individual counseling. In groups their skills or lack of skills are on display and noted and observed by students who know from their own experience what educator in their school has what it takes to help them navigate through life's problems.

Teens are smart and can quickly assess whether the counselor is up to the task at hand, ready and set. It should come as no surprise that many counselors chose to frame their helping role as a one-on-one counselor. It's safer for them and avoids the risk that comes with putting their helping skills on full display before savvy kids who have experienced many would-be helpers at school.

Counselors who choose to lead groups are a special brand. They are willing to risk putting their skills on full display and help students from every sector of the school population. For many, it's not only an act of commitment, but also one of courage. Courage in the sense that they are willing to take on the risks that come with a new role and the risk of being seen as different from other counselors. Taking on a new role can be lonely for counselors whose first priority in the school is to help students with personal problems.

Therefore any training must give aspiring group leaders the opportunity to raise their concerns and also be presented with how they would respond to issues which they have not experienced or even considered. Effective training can help provide aspiring group leaders with someone in their corner to help ready them for the realities that will be coming their way in group life. Without training, group leaders may end up failing not only their students but also themselves.

And failing to succeed at creating an effective group counseling program can have a huge cost for forward-looking guidance and counseling programs which want to help students with personal and well-being problems without adding new staff. Such a failed effort can eliminate the motivation for change and keep a guidance department stuck in a role focused solely on scheduling students for classes, testing, college admissions, and attendance and discipline counseling.

This failure will be remembered by counselors who are geared to the past and have avoided change and new programs throughout their careers as yet another example of "we've tried this kind of thing before and it never worked. Let's stick with what we know and have done for many years." These counselors know how to operate, compete, and succeed in a system that already exists and will resist any new system, such as integrating a personal counselor model into the guidance program. Effective training can help prevent a failed outcome and enable a group counseling program to gather useful data about the non-academic side of students' lives.

For example, Budd A. Moore suggested in chapter 1 that student participation in groups can be measured. In chapter 3 the author was able to demonstrate positive data about the value of group participation for the following groups in school:

- Students addicted or on the way to addiction with tobacco, alcohol, or drugs.
- Students needing support to stay tobacco-, alcohol-, and drug-free on weekends when there has been no support in the past.
- Students trying to solve grade-level developmental problems they face in grades nine, ten, eleven, and twelve.
- High-achieving students in grades eleven and twelve who are under great pressure from school staff, their parents, the community, and themselves to be standard bearers and excel no matter what the personal cost.
- Alternative high school students in need of belonging, improved self-esteem and achievement, and fewer acting-out behaviors.
- Students returning to school after referral to rehabilitation for alcohol, drugs, or tobacco addiction.
- Students who participate in mandatory counseling as a result of the use of alcohol and drugs.

But data gathering about a program's value can only come once the program has weathered the critics that are sure to arrive in the early stages. First things first. Before planning and implementing the kinds of group interventions needed in their school, counselors in training must be given the opportunity to confront and reflect on the kinds of issues and concerns they may face as group leaders.

These concerns have to be put on the table, discussed, and brought into the training process, not put on the back burner or overlooked completely. They are about to enter a professional world in which a new form of intervention is needed and they will need a different kind of compass to succeed. It's not going to be a walk in the park. All of the eyes of the school will be on the program.

That means there will be critics looking for ways to torpedo its value. To survive group leaders will need not only counseling skills but also courage, the will to win, and political, public relations, and selling skills to close the deal. Doing something different, not more of the same, can spur supporters of the status quo into battle. Group leaders and their backers should never underestimate the use of personal and professional attacks to threaten them and derail the program. Schools are often not the peaceable kingdoms they proclaim to be, nor are some of their staff peacemakers.

Some critics will not play nice. They will try to play in your sandbox and mess it up. As the author has experienced, attacks can come in many forms. Some can be personal, such as, "She's recently divorced, living with some creep, and the first one in and last one out at the Friday after-school bar scene. I'm not saying she's an alcoholic, but it's got to make you wonder about the kind of example she is setting for the school, students, and parents. Where does she get off trying to help kids with their problems when it seems she has so many of own?"

Or there can be professional attacks such as, "He's doing this group stuff because he wants to make a name for himself and become director of guidance and maybe principal someday. Look how much publicity he is bringing to himself and his program. Showoff, ambitious climber, that's who he really is, and he's using the kids to promote his career."

No one likes change, even if the system is not working and requires the current guidance program model to be disassembled in order for fundamental change to be accomplished. Like all other systems, guidance systems are organized to reproduce themselves at all costs, even when it is irrational to do so. Guidance organizations will defy change, even when they say they are changing.

The advent of a new approach like a group counseling program is often regarded by counselors who see their role as quasi-administrators as a signal to do more of the same thing they already know how to do and reject any new path being proposed. It's what they know and do well and it's home to them. They do not see what's coming. Events are not read as an indication to reassess their role and what they are doing.

However, the guidance organization they've known for many years has become insulated and self-congratulatory and is no longer able to

ignore the chasm between its practices and what is now being demanded by parents, students, some educators, and community advocates for an increase in personal counseling services.

As suggested in chapter 1, change is in the air. Given the anxiety that
change can bring, aspiring group leaders need to be emotionally prepared for the attacks that will come their way as representatives of a
new wave of counselors trained to serve as personal counselors. They
will be blamed for the problems of the old organization when the facts
suggest the opposite.

The following themes culled from the author's training programs for
group leaders can help aspiring group leaders to overcome resistance
and serve as a guide to the complexities of the issues, the opportunities,
the risks that await them, and the importance of selling the value of
their program.

In the author's experience a review and discussion of these themes
can go a long way in educating beginning group leaders on how they
can help group members become happier, healthier, and more hopeful
and successful in their lives. And of course to help themselves do the
same. Helping students to resolve their problems has a great payback
for counselors. Seeing the value of their interventions in doing good for
others can jumpstart a group leader's confidence in their mission and
work.

Here is a tutorial for beginning group leaders on the issues and skills
they need to master. One of the best ways to begin the training of
potential group leaders is by connecting the themes in group work with
students to the group leaders' own personal teenage and adult development. Many of the problems faced by group members have also been
experienced by group leaders.

Fortunately the group leader has had more experience in solving
problems and in his role as mentor and counselor he brings not only
professional but also personal life experience to the program. Recalling
his own experience in solving problems and how he was helped serves
to place him in the shoes of his students and thus enables him to walk
the talk with them as both a professional and human being. Both group
members and group leaders are connected by life's problems and as a
result have much to teach each other.

Chapter 5 will deal in more detail with how to train a potential group
leader. Here is the beginning tutorial needed to get potential group

leaders on board by connecting their own personal development with the themes in group work:

- How can groups be used to teach people better ways of caring for themselves? Have you thought about or been actually involved in self-help or other groups to improve your own self-care? What areas needed attention? Did the group experience help?
- How can groups be as inclusive of all their members as possible? Are you generally included or sometimes left out?
- Why are groups useful in helping individuals resolve past problems, accomplish present tasks, and understand future goals? How have you resolved past problems? It is not easy to do.
- Certain personal characteristics are vital to group leaders: self-awareness; genuineness; the ability for warm, caring relationships; sensitivity and understanding; self-confidence; a sense of humor; flexibility of behavior; keeping confidentiality; and willingness to self-evaluate. What are the most difficult characteristics for you? What comes easily?
- Why is the support and warmth of the leader so important? How do you assess your level of support and warmth?
- Why are group members' nonverbal responses important data? Have you given attention to the physical and emotional appearance of members and the messages their appearance is sending about who they are and what they are feeling?
- What is the best way for the group leader to pass on his or her leadership skills to members of the group so they too can play a major role in the helping process? As a group leader do you find it difficult to give up and share control with members?
- What is the best way to deal with members who resist taking part in the group process? Getting resisting members involved is no easy task. Winning members over to be real participants doesn't come easily. Their resistance is often a life-long behavior brought on by never being asked to participate and being relegated to the sidelines, an observer, and being told that their opinions and feelings don't count. As a teenager were you often forced to the sidelines, an observer, and seldom a full-fledged participant?
- Personal and professional problems hit us all. No one here escapes. In a real sense we are more alike than different. Given this

truth, why is it sometimes difficult for members to risk disclosing threatening material so they can become known for who they really are? Do you sometimes hold back from sharing problems? Could participating in this process help you to get these problems resolved?

- Often in groups, conflict emerges between members and with the group leader. Why is conflict a valuable part of the helping process in groups? How do you usually react to conflict?

- Why is honest and accurate feedback, sometimes confrontation, a valuable part of the helping process in groups? How do you usually react to confrontation? Do you use it as a helping skill? If not, what stops you? Being too nice or all-accepting can be a weakness for group leaders as this response never really challenges the members' self-erected barriers. How can you use confrontation as a positive intervention?

- Why in the process of working through a problem is it important for members to accompany insights with action? Talk is cheap, nothing changes without action. Give one example of an action you took to help resolve a problem.

- In groups active listening is a highly valued skill. Being able to hear the meaning behind words and nonverbal gestures is critical to effective communication. However active listening can be very difficult. What gets in your way when you listen to the voices and concerns of others? How would you rate your active listening? How do you go about encouraging members to be active listeners?

- Why are the realities of death and loss such strong themes in a group? How have the issues of death and loss surfaced in your life?

- We all get hit by life's problems. No one really escapes. You and the group members are no exception. Teaching members how to solve problems can be a great gift for them as they navigate through their teen years and on into adulthood. What problems and issues troubled you as a child and a teen? Were there helping groups in your school and community to turn to? What stopped you, if anything, from joining such groups?

- What are your concerns about what group members may see as barriers to participation such as privacy, confidentiality, and questions such as "Will they accept what I have to say and understand what I am feeling?" As a teen did you guard your privacy and not let your story be known to others?

Many teens don't want their story known by the whole school. Schools are not noted for maintaining privacy. In terms of your colleagues, what kind of students and problems usually get the school's and community's attention? Often the acting-out child gets the attention. In many schools groups are set up to only target students heading for academic failure or acting-out behavior.

But if we agree that every student can encounter personal problems, why do schools often ignore those students who are the best and brightest, those who show up on time, keep their mouths shut, and are nice to a fault, the so-called average kids, and those kids who are invisible, who no one cares if they show up or not. Don't these kids go through life struggling as well? Don't they need our intervention so as to better learn who they are and how to solve problems that will surely emerge? When you had problems as a teenager did the adults in the school ignore them because you were a so-called good kid who never made trouble?

- Why in our pressured school setting is there little effort to encourage students to be their brother's keeper? For example, to intervene when they see a peer heading for trouble and ask if they can help? Why aren't caring students trained in groups about simple helping techniques and credible places within the school and community to refer? Do you act as your brother's keeper in your personal and professional life? If not, what's keeping you from jumping in and connecting to those in need?
- How can groups be used in secondary schools to train students to be leaders? That is, to examine their leadership strengths and those areas that need improvement. Group training need not be limited to developing self-awareness and effective problem-solving skills. Group training can also include helping students develop more effective leadership skills. For example, learning how to become a contender, a positive model for change, and become more democratic, inclusive, caring, responsive, hopeful, and responsible.

- How do you go about the business of getting members to focus on leadership skills that are transferable to other school and community tasks? Counseling groups not only help students resolve their problems but also can show them how to help others and take on a leadership role they have long avoided, becoming contenders.
- The process of talking, hearing one's voice and being heard by others, is difficult for many students. Many students have not had the opportunity to talk about their needs, thoughts, and issues. Few people, if any, ever asked them. They lack practice in stating, "Here is what I think." Getting the words out takes great effort. It costs. They sweat and squirm, dreading the moment when they are put on the spot by an instructor, boss, or any situation that demands a response. How many of you haven't thought much about "what we want?"

We respond by saying "Whatever. I'll have what he's having." Or when the dinner comes cold, say, "It's okay, I don't want to bother them by sending it back." We need to be sensitive to each other's ability to "talk" and provide ways for each other to speak out loud as to who they are and what they want and need out of life. If student members of a group learn this valuable lesson early on their adult lives can be much happier.

- Discussing the new events in our lives in a group session provides important material for the group. Things happen to teenagers, some of them bad. A week can sometimes be an eternity when the bottom falls out in their lives. As leaders we need to be sensitive and flexible, changing our agenda and throwing out the play book when real needs emerge. Often the appearance of group members as they walk into the counseling room sends a message that trouble has visited them over the past week.

Who do you talk to when the events of the past week sometimes seem too hard to bear alone? Is there someone in your corner when troubles strike?

- Why is the process of "taking" notice of each other important in group work? To observe each member of the group and your own reaction to each group member is critical. For example, what is the demeanor, energy and confidence level, appearance, tone and quality of voice, ability to express a point of view, physical condition, hopefulness or lack of, sense of humor, sensitivity, and forms of resistance of each member?

- Which group members seemed coupled together? Are there group members who choose or are allowed to remain outside the mainstream of group interactions? Are you a good observer? Or are you too worried about how "you" are doing as a leader to take time to pause, look around, and view others?

- Being aware of the power of informal contact among group members is very important. For example noticing members in this training group who participate in short conversations before class, at the break, or after class offer support and help. Some of us are quiet helpers and supporters. That's an okay way to be. Here's an example for this training group. Greeting and welcoming fellow members at the beginning of class by letting them know that their presence counts and they are valued can be a powerful therapeutic tool.

Simple words often work best. For example, "I loved the way you helped Jim get more involved; you have great leadership skills." Simple acts of kindness, affirmations, spoken quietly help.

- The quality of the interactions you have as group leader with each group member and with the group as a whole is critical to the group's success. For example, do you tend to reach out and involve certain students more than others? Are you more comfortable with some students than others? Are you aware of this selective inclusive and non-inclusive process? Are the students aware of your comfort level with some students and lack of comfort with others? How do you plan to be more inclusive and do the necessary work to involve every member?

- In seeking help, what is your "picture" of the effective helping person? What do we look for? Here are some examples: Eyes that care? The words which encourage us to tell our story? The body stance that says, "I'm with you . . . I'm not afraid of hearing your story . . . I'm ready; tell me all that is going on." How can you develop that look, the words, the body stance which attracts, not pushes away?

- How do we help group members to follow their dreams or take a different path, when others, some they love, tell them "no" in many subtle, sometimes blunt, ways? They say, "think twice," "do what I suggest," "don't make the mistakes I made." Our response should be hopeful, yet simple. We ask them, "Where would you begin? What small step can you take? You have possibilities; let's try to take some action steps together. I'm in your corner."

Seemingly "small steps" are necessary in the change process. They represent concrete things we've done for ourselves, building blocks, one at a time, for success. How were you able to take small steps in your own life to make a needed change? Who helped you? What helping words did they use? Who refused to offer help and tried to stifle "your" needs for change? What words did they use to tear your dreams?

- How do we respond when people are in trouble and need help right away, when waiting can have serious consequences such as loss of life? What words can you speak that may motivate and convince them that now, right now, is the right time to let their cry for help be heard? In your own life were there times when you, a close family member, or friend needed help right away? What was the response to your or their cry for help?
- How do group members learn how to knock on the right door for support, to find the mother and father figure that understands, accepts, and encourages them to go on? Sometimes their own parents or guardians don't fit the caring role they need. They have to find others to fit the role. However, the path to finding an understanding adult and support can be difficult and involves lots of practice, failure, and going on, persevering.

We often go down many wrong roads in order to finally find the right one. But these caring adults are there and often close by: a teacher, coach, librarian, police person, parent of a friend, or neighbor. The group leader's network needs to include mentors who can come to the aid of kids in need and help them navigate through their difficult teen years. Do you have such a network? If not, it's time to build one.

- Learning to help others too early in life is no favor to a child. It has its costs. Sometimes having to become responsible and provide care and comfort for others such as parents, siblings, and relatives deprives us of the chance to be just a kid; to play, make mistakes, hang out, drift, and learn the skills of how to navigate through life's struggles. Learning how to take responsibility for oneself instead of everyone in need of care is not always possible when trouble strikes in a family. Circumstances can suddenly force young kids into the role of an adult caretaker overnight.

For example, often in a divorce one child takes over the responsibility as the caretaker in charge. Many of these kids fall into a life where their needs are placed second. Sometimes they even carry over their caretaker role into adulthood and become counselors and professional helpers. Even as adults their needs to play, be light, and act out are on hold. We need to be careful not to ask others to care too early, too much, too fast. They need to learn to "live" first before they become "givers."

Has this role been thrust on you early in life? What have been the consequences? How can you change your persona from being known as "just a counselor" to one of a person who is a counselor?

- Often group members need help to silence the voice in their mind that tells them "you don't belong; you're not in the club." These bully voices often gain a foothold in the minds of children who are bullied by family members, peers, and adults, even educators. They tell us our worth is questionable at best. Words can hurt. Hurtful words can last, sometimes a lifetime. Many of us know that drill. We've been told along the way we don't fit. Some of us even come to believe this feedback.

Yet there comes a time to dim these labeling voices. To say "I have arrived" or "I am on my way," let those labels and those ghosts die. Were you bullied as a child or teenager and told you weren't worthy of being part of a family or group? What was the effect on you? Are you still battling these bully words or have you found a way out? What's your story?

- How and why do people change? How do we proceed if we as leaders observe areas in which it would be helpful for our group members "to change?" As group leaders we need to keep in mind that change comes slowly and sometimes over many years. On whose shoulders is the onus for change, the group leader or the group member? It's really a combination of both. The group leader's role is to help members start on the path to change. Little steps, little changes, work best. Pushing members to change now can be asking too much of them and result in failure.

Groups leaders need to use all their skills: listening, supporting, confronting, and affirming to slowly move members along the path to change. It takes time for group members to grasp that change is possible and how they can proceed. How were you able to change as a teenager? Who helped you along the way and guided you along the path? What helping words and behaviors did they use?

- Group leadership has its own work ethos. As group leaders, we are performers. We are not unlike highly trained athletes, dancers, musicians, singers, etc. "I am ready and set" is a fitting label for successful group leaders. They are emotionally and physically ready to go. Their skills are also ready and can be called upon in different situations. They leave their own problems at the door, but don't forget how problems affect people's lives. They are focused and disciplined.

They are ready when the call comes. Talk a little about your own lifestyle. Are you ready and set emotionally and physically for the task of leading groups and helping others? What needs changing so when you enter the area of help your group members can count on you?

- Outside of the job-performing arena, how do group leaders keep themselves well, ready and set on a personal level? How do they feed and restore themselves? Effective group leadership can be draining, hard work. Do group leaders know how to play, eat well, not abuse themselves, and work at maintaining close and supportive relationships? Not easy work. Being human, we can all fall by the wayside and not be up to our best game. We are not perfect.

Group leaders experience many of the same issues of life their group members are facing. Given the reality that we all get hit by life, how do group leaders ready themselves for the call to do their work? How do they successfully handle their everyday life with all its pitfalls? And how do they stay at the top of their game by continually reassessing and learning new skills? Be up-to-date? How do you as a group leader handle your personal life? Are personal issues affecting your roles and success as a group leader? What needs changing?

However, asking members to make changes in their personal lives while you sit on the sidelines, doing nothing about your own personal issues, makes a farce out of the group leader's helping role. It becomes a "do as I say, not what I do" role. We only grow as group leaders when we, as well as our students, put in the necessary work to change. Only then are we able to understand what change is all about and what we are asking of others.

- Why is it that when group leaders follow the same formula or approach for each group it can be stifling for both the leader and group members? As a group leader one has to fight sophistication. You have to fight knowing because once you know something it's hard to be open and creative. If "we" know too much, always follow the same script, and fail to shift and adapt to new situations, then we get stuck, stale. Our model for group leadership needs to be more vibrant. Every group leader should ask "What is the point of doing what you already know?"

For example, group leaders who enter a group with a set of gimmicks meant to cover all situations don't risk much. With their focus only on control they fail to see new opportunities and learn new approaches. They only go with what they "know" and leave little opportunity for real dialogue and sharing of leadership among every group member. Are you as group leader controlling every aspect of your groups? Where do your members' ideas and participation fit?

- Why is the "selling of the value of groups" a major function for a group leader? You have to believe what you are doing is important. You really have to believe that you are of some use to your students and what you have to offer has something good for them. Let's face it; most teens don't want to change. Change is for others, not for them. So they have to be invited to the process, sold on its value, and coached as well as helped through the process. Our work is to get out among our students, sense their real needs, and create groups that can respond to "their" real needs for self-enhancement.

Waiting in the office for students to show up doesn't work. Invitations to an office, even a counselor's, usually spells trouble. And when they don't show up some counselors blame students by saying they are not interested in getting help. Case closed! However the onus is on us to create conditions in which students "want" to participate and demonstrate that through their participation they will improve their lives. The word gets around fast in schools when group leaders become knowable, their skills observable, and the groups are designed to serve the real needs of students in that particular setting.

A discussion of these themes then can serve to kick-start a training program for group counselor leaders, as the focus is on their own lives as well as those of their future group members. They are connected personally as well as professionally. It's a way to help open the door to the reality that leaders bring their own personal issues into the group experience, such as how they were helped or not helped as children, teenagers, and adults.

This chapter concludes with a number of important questions leaders need to be asked before they move into the more detailed training aspects described in chapter 5. It can be a homework lesson to reflect on as they digest the themes in chapter 4:

- How to use silence in a group to give members time to reflect on their issues and life.
- How to avoid jumping in when continued silence is called for.
- How to use confrontation in the group. Certain negative behaviors of members need to be addressed early on and reinforced. For example, consistently arriving late, talking too much, bullying others, resisting your leadership, and failing to participate can quickly lead to group deterioration. The resisters are in charge, you're not.
- How to avoid thinking you are going to ask the wrong questions. Believe you won't do damage or hurt members by what you say.

- How to quell the voice inside you that says, "I want every student in the group to like me," when you know this is unrealistic. And, as important, how do you react and deal with clients who in fact may not favor you or your work?
- How to listen and not talk "too much." That is, how to avoid preparing your own response rather than listening to the members. You can miss important data from members while you are thinking about what you are going to say.
- How to engage your members' problems. It's not enough to listen and collect material, their stories, needs, and issues, from members. You have to directly engage them with comments such as "we know you have these issues, now what is your plan to change and start down a different path?" There comes a time to ask students to take ownership and begin paying their dues.
- How to avoid dwelling on one member's problems and leave them for a time to reflect.
- How to avoid becoming "too" involved with some of your students and letting the line between professional and personal become blurred. For example, you need to keep your own needs in check. But, being human, there may come a time when your own needs for intimacy and contact begin to spill over to group members. What are the signs, the red lights that may signal you are becoming "too" involved?
- How can I reveal myself, become knowable, to my group without becoming the focus of the group? How available should I become to group members?
- How do you or should you "hide" your own uneasiness and nervousness in leading a group?
- Sometimes you may fear that as a group leader you could lead members down a "wrong path" by giving bad advice. How do you avoid a pattern of giving advice to your members? Yet there are some times that direct advice is needed. What are some examples?
- In terminating a group, it is important for group members to give you direct feedback on your performance as a group leader, on areas you do well and skills that need improvement. How good are you at accepting feedback from group members?

- How do you deal with your feelings that members will not relate to you because they think you are too old, too young, and out of date, not with it?

- Sometimes when the group process hits a snag you may become uneasy that members and colleagues will see you as a fraud or question your skills and knowledge base. How do you instill in yourself the feeling that you are well trained, have something to offer members that is useful to them, and need to be taken seriously? You are a doer and need to believe that and prove it to others.

- Failure is a part of the professional life. We don't succeed with every member and every group. Sometimes the fit isn't there. How are you going to resolve counseling relationships that don't work out? Keep in mind that each intervention to help may still have value, even a failed one. Getting help and changing one's life is often an incremental process. Many failed interventions can lead to a successful one.

- On the other hand, sometimes we think we can save the world. You are the standard bearer, ready and set to right the wrongs you see being inflicted on your members. Should we try to change those feelings? Maybe you are not God, just a human being trying to make a small, positive dent in members' lives.

- Sometimes others may see you as an all-perfect helper, up to helping every member resolve any problem that comes his way. But in reality you are not so perfect and skilled as others may think. How do I reach out to colleagues for help and let them know I am not always the right person at the right time to handle the most difficult members and groups?

- Why is it that sometimes we resist learning new leadership and helping behaviors that will enable us to become more effective professionals? We tend to stay with behaviors that we know, that we are comfortable with, even though they may not be working. Giving up these outmoded behaviors is not easy. It's what we know. We resist change even though the change will help us to be more effective leaders. Moving from what we know and trying on new leadership behaviors is hard work. An important part of our work is to learn that resistance is a positive and necessary ingredient when people begin to change. While it's the first step, we need to find a way to move beyond these barriers and take the risk to learn new approaches.

- Why is there often a depressed feeling for group leaders after a helping group ends? That is true for leaders as well as members. Group members spend a number of intense hours together. Relationships get formed, sometimes after a stormy give and take. We live fully in the period, not sure of the outcome or destination. In returning to the world, our lives seem less risky and exciting. We are back to business as usual, it seems. But it doesn't have to be that way. How do you plan to hold on to the zest and love for living you have fostered in this group?

- Why is there an effort for a few group leaders to continue a connection with group members after termination, an effort to keep things as they were? We all want to hang on to connections that matter. What is it you think you are going to miss most about this group? Why do some counselors "hang on to relations with members," even though they know they should let go? It's often a sign that their personal needs are not being met and that they are using their role as group leader to meet these needs. As leaders we should follow the advice we give group members: identify your own needs, reflect on what's missing, and take the necessary action steps required to meet these needs. Simply put, group leaders need to be aware when they are using, perhaps abusing, the group experience and group members to meet their personal needs.

This awareness should ignite a red light of danger signaling the need to back off and seek counsel from a colleague or professional. This behavior is not uncommon for group leaders and, as suggested in chapter 5, it needs to be addressed not only for group leaders but also for the members they are entrusted to care for. Group leaders need to avoid becoming friends or parent figures, or carrying on intimate relationships with members. A professional divide must be maintained or mischief can take place. More on this often unspoken, overlooked, and kept secret issue in chapter 5.

KEY IDEAS

- In this chapter the report of the actual group counseling program speaks for itself. The author believes the reader can gain more insight into why this program was successful by exploring the organizational and political dynamics, the backdrop of this story, which enabled the program to emerge and be successful. An understanding of these dynamics will help future group leaders be better prepared for the subtle aspects that emerge when there is a need for change and new programs such as group counseling in guidance programs.
- When many parents, community members, students, and educators think of counselors and what they do, they view the counselor's role as focusing almost entirely on overseeing mandated testing programs, scheduling students for classes, and counseling for college admissions, attendance, and discipline problems. Counseling students for personal problems is seen as a low priority, utilized when time permits, which is often never, or offered by other support services.
- Responsibility for personal counseling has moved out of the guidance office and is now in the hands of a dwindling number of social workers and school psychologists, whose services are spread over many schools in a district due to budget cuts. A student in crisis may have to wait hours for a psychologist to arrive. Counseling interventions for kids and parents in need are not available in many schools in spite of the school districts' claims to not let one student fall between the cracks.
- Efforts to return the personal counseling role to guidance departments are often met with resistance by counselors who prefer the quasi-administrator role which emphasizes the counselor as an expert and data manager on testing, placement of students in classes, college admissions, student attendance, and discipline issues. In many schools the guidance department has become an ancillary service of the school administration rather than an intervention system for students. This is the mindset that defines guidance programs in today's schools and must be changed.
- As a result, while there is an increase in students arriving at the schoolhouse door with personal problems, the present way guidance departments are organized, with their emphasis on administrative tasks, limits the availability of counselors to offer personal counseling

intervention. A major cause for this limit on personal counseling outreach is not only the resistance of quasi-administrative counselors to this role but also because counselors are often assigned to students by either grade level or alphabet rather than according to the counseling skills they possess. This model for deploying counselors is flawed and at the root of the problems facing guidance organizations in today's schools. It is flawed because the model suggests all counselors are created equal and able to address any problem that students bring them. It ignores the reality that some counselors are administratively oriented and interested in those tasks while other counselors arrive at the counseling department with skills and interests in offering personal counseling interventions.

- Unfortunately those counselors with interest and skills in personal counseling seldom get to use their skills for three reasons. One, they work in an organization that is clerically and administratively oriented and are left with little time to do personal counseling. Two, there is great pressure on them to go along with the present system if they expect to be tenured and supported by their fellow counselors. That means putting their personal counseling ambitions and skills aside and being a cooperative part of the existing system and team. In other words, if you want tenure, play in our sandbox, do what we do, and like it. Three, as long as counselors are assigned to students by alphabet or grade rather than counseling skills they will never be able to reach their goal of being a full-time personal counselor for students.

- As this chapter describes, this organizational model for deploying counselors can be changed by assigning counselors based on personal counseling skills or quasi-administrative skills. The author developed this model at Shoreham-Wading River High School, where he became a personal counselor with the title of student assistance counselor and held a full-time position to offer group and individual counseling and serve as a trainer for students, staff, and parents. The remaining members of the guidance department focused entirely on an administrative role which they were interested in and familiar with.

- This differentiation of staff made way for the development of the successful group counseling program at Shoreham. An intervention probably would not have seen the light of day in a system where counselors with skills and interest in personal counseling are never able to find their niche. This model was able to emerge because of the backing of key administrators, staff, parents, and school board members who realized that the high school had to respond to the growing personal problems of students in new ways. To begin with there had to be a reorganization of the guidance department to utilize the intervention skills of a well-trained counselor who would take over interventions for students and parents and create a supportive environment, safety net, and circle of wellness by training teachers, students, and parents as advisers and helpers.

- As this chapter notes, what followed this organizational change was a sense of relief for counselors, administrators, staff, students, and parents. They could breathe a sense of relief feeling at last that they had found a workable intervention system. They felt relief that finally school counselors would be able to do what they do best and put a stop to the ongoing complaints that the administration and counselors weren't doing enough to help students at risk. In this new arrangement the signs for where to get help would shine bright and clear. There would be no confusion concerning which door to open for counseling help and guidance information.

- As a result of this organizational change the guidance department would now be in a position to gather data on the number of students being counseled for personal problems, the kinds of problems they were experiencing, the kinds of interventions utilized, and the results of this intervention. Finally there would be accountability to make sure the counseling department was serving students in need as well as providing data on testing, college admissions, class placement, and attendance and discipline interventions. This was to be the new model and mindset for the guidance department. Now when the district's public relations publication stated "we will let no student fall between the cracks," it would be true.

- Finally, while this successful group counseling program was fortunate to have the backing of key educators and parents, it still had to be sold as a needed intervention to parents, administrators, students, teachers, support staff, and community advocates. They had to understand and visualize how personal counseling interventions could help their children and students. Every parent and student knows the value of a good teacher or administrator and what they mean to a student's success. What is needed for counselors to be successful in today's school world is an ongoing effort, a sell, and a clear model to demonstrate the value of personal counseling interventions and how they work. A group counseling program can be the beginning of an effort to win or bring back personal counseling interventions to where they first started and belong: the guidance and counseling department.

5

TRAINING COUNSELORS AS
GROUP LEADERS

The author has been involved for over thirty years in leading school intervention groups and training counselors to be successful group leaders for middle school, junior high, and high school students. He has served as a counselor at the middle school, junior high, and high school levels, as a high school student assistance counselor, and as a district director of guidance. He holds a PhD in counselor education with special emphasis on preparing counselors for group work.

The author has also taught classes in graduate-level counselor education programs which included teaching the following group courses to prepare students to lead groups in their schools: group approaches; theories and practices; group counseling laboratory, which included practical group counseling experiences and the counseling of their own groups; and advanced group counseling laboratory, with a focus on effective group counseling leadership.

The training program offered here represents the best practices of the author's body of work in training counselors to be group leaders. Counselors need to know themselves well, their strong points as potential group leaders, and the areas that need improvement before they enter real group life. Effective training can make the difference between success and failure for both the counselor and his students.

Here are the necessary steps to prepare counselors as group leaders:

STEP ONE: HELPING COUNSELORS UNDERSTAND
THE PURPOSE OF GROUPS

Effective groups have many purposes. For example, to offer the counseling process to a larger number of students; to teach group members
problem-solving skills; to teach group members to better understand
their dark sides, or those issues that cause them to erect barriers to
certain people and groups; to teach group members to better accept
and understand people who may be different in terms of gender, sexual
orientation, physical and mental abilities, personality, culture, color,
age, etc.; or to teach group members that as human beings we are more
alike than different.

They can also teach group members that we all get hit by life. No
one is immune to life's problems. Group members learn how to use
their helping and leadership skills in assisting others; learn that in the
process of helping others they in turn help themselves; are encouraged
to develop lifestyles in which they shine their own light and become
useful and contributing members of the community; and teach group
leaders the need to pass on their helping skills to other members of the
community in order to establish a community-wide helping network.

STEP TWO: HELPING COUNSELORS UNDERSTAND
THE STAGES OF GROUP DEVELOPMENT

Counselors in training need to understand that groups have beginning,
work, and ending stages. For example, there is a beginning stage in
which the first priority of the group leader is to establish a safe and
caring environment in which members begin to know each other and at
the same time plant the seeds for self-disclosure and risk taking. Little
things mean a lot in this stage.

For example, it is important that the group leader know members'
names, the issues and concerns they bring into the group, the helping
skills that work well for them and those that need improvement, and
what resources/skills they can offer to other group members.

The middle stage of the group focuses on "the work" of the group.
That is to help individual members begin to resolve some of the issues
that brought them into the group. In this stage, the helping skills of

group members and leaders are highlighted. Members begin to understand that in the process of helping others, they gain better self-understanding and problem-solving skills.

In the final stage, group members learn how to assess their own skills and problem-solving development and those areas and skills that need more attention. In this process, members play a key role in offering feedback to each other. The group leader also plays a major role by offering his assessment of each member and his or her performance. Finally, members and the group leaders address the issues of termination, loss, and moving out.

In the process, members and group leaders learn firsthand what it's like to be part of a group's ending. This stage of group development serves to remind group leaders that their work as group leaders is not only to create a safe and caring climate that helps members learn to be more effective persons, but also to let members "go" and move on to help others.

In a sense, the work of the group leader is similar to that of a choreographer, pulling together the needs and concerns of the group members so they become clear, coherent, and accessible to work on. As group leaders, we are trying to find the right rhythm and style that fits a particular group. It's an ongoing process of assessment.

As such, one of the key elements in our leadership style is our ability to hold meaningful conversations with each group member and the total group. That is to talk and listen in ways that make sense to them. Yes, as group leaders we sometimes feel we will run out of questions, be forced into silence, and that the group will drift. That's true for all leaders and performers in music, the arts, sports, etc. We need to recognize these feelings and fears that "we will be running on empty" and let them percolate. They help to sharpen our focus.

STEP THREE: LEADING HELPING GROUPS REQUIRES A DIFFERENT MODEL THAN TEACHING STUDENTS

Leading groups is not "teaching." In the group leadership role we are not trying to "teach" members about issues such as death and loss, stress, suicide, or alcohol and drug abuse. We use a leadership model that relies heavily on the involvement, participation, response, and use of the helping skills of "each member," not only the group leaders. Leading a group does not require a detailed, step-by-step, textbook lesson that has been planned ahead and leaves out the particular issues that concern the present members.

In fact, too many canned lessons and too much leader-led structure are often counterproductive in groups. Why? Too much time consumed with lecturing, irrelevant activities, and leader-led busy work to control the group can rob participants of the necessary time and opportunity to talk, tell their own stories, and learn from the stories of others. And that process can also rob leaders of the valuable experience of simply focusing on each participant rather than on their own pre-planned agenda.

An agenda, while on the surface done with good intentions, in reality may be an effort to calm the leader's anxiety, fears of "If I don't plan each minute, what will I do?" and fears of failure and client resistance. All are normal reactions, as we are all human. However, though we may need some kind of structure to begin a session, the major part of our group sessions should focus on creating conditions and "space" for the involvement of participants.

We also need to keep in mind that the work in leading a group is not all the leader's responsibility. In fact, when participants are asked to share their experiences and be involved, and when their contributions are valued, the group becomes a group-directed learning experience where the "learning" comes from the entire group, not from the leader alone. It becomes a process in which each member, not just the leader, is encouraged and expected to make a contribution that is personal, not abstract. Therefore, the main goal is to help participants become aware of how these issues have affected their personal lives, family members, and peers.

When we move into the schools our leadership role in both individual and group counseling needs to focus on a model that stresses inviting and welcoming, creating conditions for teens to feel safe and accepted, encouraging them to tell their story, hear their own voices, and in the process help them find their own alternatives and solutions, with our support. The bottom line is kids need to know that the problems they are trying to resolve are not unique to them. Hearing the stories of peers and learning how they cope and resolve similar issues can be a powerful helping tool.

As counselors, our role is to provide some arena of comfort in which kids can feel relaxed and comfortable, where their problems can be viewed as more normal than different, where they can become reinvigorated and begin to learn how to change the discomfort and pain that exists in other parts of their lives. You can't teach group members about freedom. They have to feel, see, and experience it at an emotional as well as intellectual level.

Telling them how they should proceed to free themselves from their problems doesn't work. What works is helping them figure out the necessary steps to "free" themselves and supporting them as they encounter resistance, setbacks, failures, and hopefully some successes, in the work to change their lives.

However there is a scarcity of groups in secondary schools to help teens resolve personal and well-being problems that they encounter in their normal development. What we have instead are "teaching groups" in which counselors teach students about such topics as college admissions, scholarship, financial aid, career choice, and course selection. These structured groups are set up to carry out the mission of the school to give students facts and information.

These are important and useful group activities that are needed by many students. But they do not address the reality that many teenagers are searching for an open door for help and support to solve non-academic problems, and in many schools they find only closed doors. Counseling groups can provide the open door for these needy students and help them learn how to successfully navigate through the pitfalls of adolescent life.

We also need to keep in mind that the group leadership role modeled here is one of a facilitator. As facilitator, the group leader seeks to support and empower group members as individuals and as a group in pursuing their growth and learning. The leader acts as a stimulus and resource rather than as an expert, working to create an environment in which each group member's ability to manage themselves and contribute to one another's growth and learning is supported.

In this model the leader expects group members to reap the benefits of increased self-esteem associated with taking increased responsibility for, and initiative in, pursuit of their own growth and learning.

STEP FOUR: BEING AWARE OF THE HAZARDS AND RISKS INVOLVED IN CLOSE CONTACT WITH NEEDY ADOLESCENTS

It is important to raise the awareness of aspiring group counselors about the hazards and risks of becoming too involved with their needy students. Some students come into the counseling process looking for a personal relationship with a mature adult figure. And that adult figure is often a counselor. As a result, the close contact that accompanies group interaction can present some risks for both the leader and needy group members.

In the author's experience this important issue is ignored and left out of a counselor's training to lead helping groups. Unfortunately, it is a taboo subject in the many schools where the culture turns a blind eye to the possibility of school staff being involved in sexual misconduct and prides itself on naively thinking, "These kinds of problems don't happen here."

As a result, both staff members and their needy students may be at risk of sexual misconduct and end up destroying their lives. Effective training can minimize this risk. Therefore, it is critical that clear boundaries be established concerning the group leader's relationships with group members. The counselor must establish his role as a professional dedicated to helping members resolve their problems and not become their friend, parent figure, or in some cases, a messiah figure out to dominate and control their personal lives.

That role requires the building of the following boundaries and the development of an internal warning system, a red light signaling alarm, if the counselor finds himself avoiding these boundaries and putting himself and a group member at risk of sexual misconduct. Here are some examples of the necessary boundaries of which group leaders need to remind themselves:

- He is not their parent, friend, or companion.
- He interacts with his group members only during school hours as a group leader and one-on-one counselor.
- He does not take group members out to lunch.
- He does not interact socially with group members after school hours.

- He does not carry on email, twitter, texting, or phone conversations with group members.

Using the author's Counselor Sexual Misconduct Awareness Inventory[1] is a good place to start in helping aspiring counselors raise their awareness about the downside of too-close personal conduct without boundaries. Here is the inventory:

Counselor Sexual Misconduct Awareness Inventory: Part One

This inventory will help raise your awareness about the issue of sexual misconduct. Your answers and observations are important, as they will provide material for our discussions. Please try to answer each question:

1. As counselors we are all attracted to certain students. For example, these may be students you feel a special closeness to and want to spend more time with. We all have our "favorite" students. Please describe these students and what makes them special in your eyes.
2. Effective counselor-student relationships go two ways. Counselors as well as students receive something of value from such relationships. What are you getting in return from students to whom you feel close and consider special?
3. When you were a teenager, was there a staff person to whom you felt close, who made you feel special, and with whom you wanted to spend more time?
4. Are you attracted to helping students with certain kinds of problems? This might be a student affected by a troubled home life, a divorce or separation, a death or serious illness in the family, alcohol and drug addiction in the family, violence, school failure, poor peer relationships, eating disorders, potential suicides, or physical, emotional, or sexual abuse. Please describe these students and your feelings toward them.
5. When you were a teenager, did you experience some of these same problems in your life? Briefly describe these problems and their impact on your counseling style now.
6. Do you ever consider taking some of these "problem" students home so they could have a better life, be safe, and be cared for?

Have you taken on the role of surrogate parent, remembering their birthdays, checking on their lives outside of school, even meeting them after school for conferences?

7. Have there been occasions when you had to draw a clear line, a boundary, between yourself and students who wanted a close relationship such as that of a friend, savior, surrogate parent, or even lover? Please describe these situations and what made you sense you might be beginning to cross a professional boundary.

8. How did you distance yourself from these students? Did you remain in their lives as a caring counselor by setting some kind of workable boundary? Or did you find yourself ignoring the students' advances completely?

9. Did you ever talk, or want to talk, to a colleague, supervisor, friend, or family member about how to avoid becoming too involved in a student's personal life and problems while at the same time being an effective counselor? Please describe your feelings.

10. Did you ever observe a fellow counselor becoming too involved with a student? What was your reaction? Did you approach this counselor and share your concern that he or she might be crossing a professional boundary? Or did you consider it none of your business? Please describe your reaction when you observe a colleague beginning to cross professional boundaries and becoming a friend, savior, or surrogate parent to a student.

11. In most cases of sexual misconduct, colleagues and administrators tend to look the other way when they observe staff members becoming too involved with students. Unfortunately, this leaves the staff member and student involved on their own and sometimes results in a love relationship that leaves both parties scarred for life. Why do you think colleagues and administrators are hesitant to confront such behavior and direct the staff member and student to sources of help before it is too late?

12. What are your feelings about staff members who cross professional boundaries and become too involved with their students?

13. Do you think sexual misconduct happens only with male staff members and female students? Do you think female staff members can become involved with male students or that there are homosexual relationships that are often underreported?

14. Can you imagine a situation when you might become involved in crossing professional boundaries with a student? After all, you are human and have needs for affection. Sometimes our professional guard does come down. Describe a possible scenario in which you might unwittingly become involved because of your good intentions to help a student.

15. To whom would you turn for help and advice if you found yourself heading for a friend, savior, or parent surrogate role with a student?

16. Conversely, how would you respond, what would you say if a colleague came to you asking for help and advice on how to separate him or herself from a deepening personal relationship with a student?

17. How would you describe "effective professional boundaries" that allow you to become involved in close relationships with students but at the same time offer a barrier, a layer of protection, from becoming too involved?

Counselor Sexual Misconduct Awareness Inventory: Part Two

In the second section of the CSMAI you will be asked to complete a series of checklists. These checklists will help you to develop a more in-depth awareness about the issues involved in sexual misconduct such as the student problems that attract our attention, common hazards and risks for teachers involved in close contact with students, and self controls that help us to erect workable boundaries.

Check the student groups and problems you tend to get too involved with:

_____ Gifted and talented students
_____ Student athletes
_____ Male students
_____ Female students
_____ Gay and lesbian students
_____ Students with handicaps
_____ Average students
_____ Special education students
_____ College-bound students

_____ Minority students

_____ Acting-out students

_____ Students who abuse alcohol

_____ Students who abuse drugs

_____ Students who abuse tobacco

_____ Students returning from rehab

_____ Students whose parents are separated or divorced

_____ Students who have experienced the death or serious illness of
a family member/friend

_____ Students who are school failures and potential dropouts

_____ Students who have an eating disorder such as anorexia or
bulimia

_____ Students who have suicidal thoughts or have made suicide
attempts

_____ Students who have experienced physical, emotional, or sexual
abuse

_____ Students with poor peer relationships

_____ Students with troubled home relationships

Please check those items that you feel represent hazards and risks for
counselors involved in close relationships with students:

_____ The counselor holds more than one meeting a week with a
certain student.

_____ Other students complain that their meeting time is being cut
back.

_____ The counselor switches meetings with the student to late
afternoon or evening.

_____ The counselor begins to hold meetings outside the school at a
local diner or the student's home.

_____ The counselor is flattered by the student's interests in his or
her personal life.

_____ The counselor buys the student presents for birthdays and
special events.

_____ The counselor writes the student letters of encouragement on
a regular basis.

_____ The counselor accompanies the student on field trips.

_____ The counselor drives the student back and forth to school.

_____ The counselor spends time with the student at dances and school activities.

_____ The counselor requests that the student be added to his counseling load.

_____ The student's parents become concerned about the counselor's over-involvement with their child.

_____ The student's teachers and administrators begin to ask questions about the counselor's over-involvement with the student.

Counselors can avoid the hazards and risks involved in helping by controlling the where, when, and how of the helping process. Here is a checklist of "Don'ts."

Please check any item that might present a hazard for you:

_____ Don't drive students to school or home alone.

_____ Don't take a student out to breakfast, lunch, or dinner.

_____ Don't buy a student gifts for birthdays or other special occasions.

_____ Don't limit your social life to students and school activities.

_____ Don't limit your need for an ego boost and flattery to students.

_____ Don't shortchange some students by depriving them of an equal amount of meeting time.

_____ Don't write personal letters to students on a regular basis.

_____ Don't hold helping meetings outside of school.

_____ Don't hold helping meetings in the late afternoon or evening.

The CSMAI can be very helpful in motivating counselors to talk about their own search for how to set boundaries and establish a protective barrier they can invoke when the counselor-student relationship becomes too intimate. The inventory helps to create conditions in which counselors, often for the first time, can voice their concerns about close relationships with students and identify sources of support they can turn to. Here are some examples of counselors' concerns and sources of guidance:

- Learning how to set boundaries usually occurs on the counselor's own watch. In most cases he or she has no training and little supervision on how to proceed. It is a hit-or-miss situation.
- The help counselors do receive often comes from a counselor who voluntarily serves as a big brother or sister to show them how to behave in close relationships with students.
- Many counselors are aware that they have favorite students whom they seek out, but at the same time they are bothered by this behavior. They often feel unprofessional when behaving like this and think that they are depriving other students of their needed attention.
- Many counselors feel a strong emotional tug to help students with difficult personal problems but fear they may be being drawn into unknown, even dangerous, territory.
- Counselors are also confused when needy students demand more of their attention and many lack skills in how to say "no" or "I can't." The word "frozen" seems to capture their feelings and behavior.
- In terms of sharing thoughts about being attracted to a student, counselors tend to keep those feelings to themselves or confide in a colleague, friend, or family member outside of school. They feel it could be harmful to their career and job security to share their thoughts with an administrator.
- They have observed colleagues becoming too involved with students but generally feel it is not their job to intervene.
- Counselors with troubled home lives are often looking for the opportunity to confide in a colleague and share the burden of how these troubles are affecting their counselor performance.

This inventory can serve the purpose of bringing the subject of the hazards and risks of too-close involvement with needy students out of the closet and into the open for dialogue. Group counselors do worry about their role and their own well-being when they find themselves becoming too involved with a group member.

Questions about close contact come with the territory and counselors need a place to share their concerns and receive helpful feedback, guidance, and support. The inventory can help group counselors identify sources of help they can trust when they find themselves crossing boundaries and becoming too involved. These might include a close colleague, therapist, family member, or mentor such as a former professor.

This is another example of how effective training can prepare counselors and other professionals to think ahead and consider their reaction about issues that they do not see on the horizon. Better to be prepared than, as in the case of sexual misconduct, naively think it can't happen in my school and it certainly can't happen to me or a colleague.

STEP FIVE: USING THE GROUP LEADERS SELF-AWARENESS INVENTORY TO PERSONALIZE THE TRAINING PROCESS

The Group Leaders Self-Awareness Inventory[2] was developed by the author to help make aspiring group leaders more aware of their skills, their lack of skills, the students they embrace, and the students they avoid. It's an important tool in helping counselors move from a safe level of reading about group leadership into considering critical aspects of how they view their role as helpers.

Completing the inventory is an important step in analyzing the counselor's skills as a potential group leader. The inventory will also help them focus on those leadership areas in which they need improvement. In addition, this exercise can help them focus on the kinds of personalities, problems, and issues they tend to gravitate to and those they choose to avoid or push away. This is valuable data that needs to be brought to the surface, as we, in our daily personal and professional interaction, are continuously involved in groups.

Only serving people whom we like, relate to, and feel comfortable with and staying clear of others whom we see as "different" and who raise our level of discomfort can render us ineffective and self-serving. Every professional leader has a dark side that creates barriers to help with certain groups and people. Ongoing self-assessment is vital as taking on barriers to different groups and people can find a home in our counseling repertoire.

Our work is to shine some light on that dark side, not be afraid of it, as it is a human condition, and develop the communication skills needed to interact successfully with those who stir something inside our souls that makes us want to flee. Finally, the inventory provides needed material, a glimpse into our own stories for simulating real group experience. We all arrive here having lived a life. We have experienced joys and successes as well as failures and despair. We've encountered loss, abuse, and addiction in our relationships.

We all get hit by life. Hopefully completing the inventory will show that we are coupled as a group and more alike than different. Each of us brings a story to be told, dreams that need encouragement and support, dark roads and experiences that need new light and resolution, self-erected barriers that need dismantling, and positive contact that can restore our energy and ready us for the problems and issues that the world is certain to lay at our doorstep.

Group Counselors Self-Awareness Inventory

The purpose of this exercise is to help you assess your strengths as a helper. The following questions will help you focus on the kinds of problems and people that elicit your best helping efforts. It will also help you to identify areas that are more difficult for you and need shoring up.

- What events or influences led you to want to help others?
- Who are your models and mentors? What did they teach you about the helping process? In particular, what words and actions did they use that made them stand out as effective helpers?
- Have you modeled your professional life after some of these valued mentors? Do you use some of the same skills or words you learned from these mentors in your own helping role? Can you still hear their voices?
- Often in our own development as persons and professionals, we encounter helpers who are ineffective. While well-meaning, they lack the skills, sometimes even the interest, to be effective helpers. They often use words and actions that send a signal that you had better look elsewhere. Can you still hear their voices? Do you work to not become like them yourself? Please describe how these would-be helpers may have impacted your life. They missed an opportunity. Did it hurt?

- What are your personal goals in helping others? In other words, what's in it for you? What do you think you will gain from the process?
- What are your fears about the helping process? We all come into the helping process a little uneasy. Questions abound. Will there be problems you feel you can't handle? Will your uneasiness with some clients come through?
- What kinds of people and groups do you prefer to help? In spite of the wise advice in our training that we need to be inclusive, we are still human and often our response is to maintain our own level of comfort. We tend to gravitate toward certain people and groups to help, those who don't threaten our professional and personal comfort zone. Given this reality, we need to be aware of this tendency, and see it clearly, so we don't avoid "the other" who may unsettle us. We need to constantly reassess our level of inclusion and work to expand, not limit, those we embrace. For example, do you like to help women, men, the elderly, younger people, the well-educated, the economically well-off, the needy, the underdog, those left out of the mainstream, victims, etc.? Whom do you gravitate toward?
- What kinds of people and groups do you prefer not to help? We all have a dark side. We have a life experience in which we have been told to stay clear of some people and groups. The influence of our parents, peers, community, and culture may have placed limits on those whom we include and value. We are not always inclusive. For example, have you erected barriers with some clients because of age, gender, culture, color, personality, ethnicity, appearance, etc? Whom do you avoid? Does it show?
- What kinds of problems interest you and motivate you to want to help? Again, our own background and experience often influence us to want to help with certain problems. For example, these might be problems with relationships, divorce, a gambling addiction, finances, abuse, loss and loneliness, anger and violence, etc. What is your preferred problem list?
- What kinds of problems do you tend to avoid, refer to others, or bluntly say, "I don't do these kinds of problems?" For example, do you avoid suicide, health issues such as anorexia and bulimia, ex-

tramarital affairs, grieving, etc? What is your "I don't want to deal with this" list?

- List your strengths as a helper. For example, are you an effective listener? Questioner? Are you nonjudgmental? Knowable? Able to confront when necessary? Do you know when to end the counselor-student relationship and move on? Are you able to establish a trusting and accepting relationship? Are you able to refer to and seek the advice of a colleague or mentor when necessary?

- At the same time, we all have areas in which we lack skills or have skills that need improvement. We can never become consummate professionals without addressing these areas. Using a baseball analogy, we are like a pitcher who, while he has a good fastball, lacks a curve and a change-up. What skills do you lack? Do you need to learn to be less judgmental? A better listener? Must you learn to engage problems you now avoid or refer to someone else? Confront when necessary? Learn when to end a helping relationship rather than holding on to it to satisfy your own personal need for belonging and communication?

- How do you view yourself as a professional helper? Are you good at this work or just getting along?

- How do others view you as a professional helper? For example, do colleagues see you as effective? What about your students and their parents? Your family members and friends? Do they value your helping skills?

- Effective helpers often have an informal support group of people with whom they can talk, receive and give feedback, and sound off about their professional and personal issues. It should come as no surprise that our professional and personal issues sometimes get meshed together. After all, when we help others we often become aware of our own personal issues that need attention. They persist and cry out for action. We are not immune to problems and we suffer the same setbacks and problems that our students face. We are not much use to our students if we are not working at resolving our own personal issues. To keep ourselves on an even keel, we need trusted colleagues and friends who can give us honest and sometimes harsh and unpleasant feedback. List at least ten people who currently serve, or could serve, as a support group for you. These are people who are available to you, make time for you, and are concerned about your personal and professional development. These people know your dark side and can quickly zero in when you are heading for conflict.

The inventory can yield important data about how aspiring group leaders view their skills, their lack of skills, and their fit to be effective group leaders. Here's an example. What follows are responses from master-level counselor education students who took the Group Leaders Self-Awareness Inventory as part of a course on group leadership taught by the author.

As the reader can observe, these responses reveal their issues and concerns, the help and rejection they have experienced developing as persons from professional helpers, and the skills and experience they are seeking to be effective group leaders. The responses also provide a road map of their specific needs for further training that can be incorporated into an ongoing training program. Here are the responses:

- I need work on how to confront when necessary.
- When I attended high school my guidance counselor did absolutely nothing for me except schedule. I want to be a more positive influence to younger kids.
- When professionals make mockingly inappropriate comments about students, I am concerned about the impact on them.
- I want to help others because I understand drug addiction and alcoholism. There are always those that can't help themselves. I wish to be there for others to listen to them as others have listened to me.
- My parents were divorced when I was fourteen; I always tried to play mediator, especially with mom and my brother.
- During high school I was lucky to have an excellent guidance counselor who showed me it was possible to connect with students.
- If I became as effective as Dr.____, I would consider myself a true professional. Yes! I still hear her voice.
- I am concerned about taking on the responsibility of others and their problems.
- The one thing I really need to work on is the emotional work. I tend to focus on the problems and only touch on the emotions.

- In terms of modeling, one of the professors taught me to have my students repeat something they said so they could hear themselves.
- I've learned through my mother's mistakes to not be too self-sacrificing and the importance of emotional and physical boundaries.
- I hear my high school counselor's voice because I am interning in her office now. I am trying to get a sense of how she does it because she seems very relaxed and effective.
- I feel I don't know how to step away as a helper.
- My high school guidance counselor was very ineffective with me. The one time I really had to talk to my counselor I was shoved away by the secretary. I remember how much that hurt.
- I become consumed with the need to find solutions instead of enabling someone to find their own solutions.
- I will definitely model my professional life after Mr. _____. I definitely use his words and techniques when I conduct groups and one-to-one counseling sessions and always hear his voice; it is with me all the time.
- I believe that every human being has a moral obligation to help someone in need.
- Things involving sexual abuse and rape might give me trouble.
- I've had the experience of being counseled several years ago. I have to say the counselor missed the boat. Actually, she was very unethical. When I tried to terminate she made it very difficult for me, but I got away.
- When I was in college my pitching coach for baseball was not an effective helper for any member of the team. All he wanted was a paycheck. His bullying had a negative impact on my life and I ended up quitting. I never want to yell and criticize kids and think I am helping them.
- My fears are that I may innocently miss signs coming from someone that I need to help.
- I am afraid I will give bad advice, that perhaps people will misinterpret what I mean. I may also become flustered when speaking, trying to find the right words to express what I want to say.
- I had a professor that I would avoid at all costs. This professor was very judgmental toward us students and the kids we were re-

quired to work with in our counselor internship. I feel she crossed the line in her opinions about things that students shared in class. It hurt very much, as she judged me as well as my family in front of the entire class.

- I totally lack a mushy side. I like to be sincere and real. I'm not good at expressing the "warm fuzzies" or the "Let's have a hug." I have a meat-and-potatoes approach to problem solving and sometimes that puts people off.

- I sometimes feel the need to provide answers rather than just listen to someone's problems.

- I think suicide and grieving problems are hard to deal with.

- The worst leaders are the ones who never stop talking. They use the word "I" more often than they should, and they don't value the experiences and input of others. Yes, I do work to not become like them, and people, especially my co-worker, tend to seek me out when they have an issue that needs to be addressed.

- My personal goal is for students to know they are not alone. I want my office to be a place of comfort and security.

- I think the skill I lack is confronting problems. I'm very hesitant in doing this because my personality is a quiet one and likes to avoid confrontation.

- My fears in the helping process are that I will lead them to bad advice.

- I've gotten so much better with being nonjudgmental as well as listening more. When divorce topics are presented, I tend to put my experiences on the table.

- I don't think I could effectively help people who are close to death. I am fairly uncomfortable with those situations. I also think I would have difficulty helping young children who may not understand how the counseling relationship works.

- I fear that each time I'm confronted with a problem that I've never handled before I'll experience some anxiety and nervousness. I hope that if I do feel uneasy that I'll be able to conceal it when I'm with my student.

- The event that influenced me to help others was my divorce and becoming a single parent.

- What's in the role of counselor for me? I also feel that I will learn more about myself as a person through this process.

- I know I'm not going to make a lot of money, but what I would like to achieve is to help individuals feel good about themselves.
- I might have trouble counseling a person who is deeply depressed.
- In terms of fears about the helping process, first is the whole confidence issue. I know that will ease with time.
- I seem to gravitate towards students in need, students whose parents don't seem involved in their life. Sometimes I want to give them that hug they so need and let them know they have found a person who cares. However, I also know that I can't.
- Here are some problems that I will not handle calmly or gracefully: (1) child abuser/molester; (2) an alcoholic, especially one who sees no problem with drinking and driving.
- Confrontation is a problem, because I hate to hurt people's feelings.
- I have to learn not to take things so personally. I let many things upset me and I cannot just let them go. I need to learn to deal with things and move on.
- One of the fears I have is that I will run into the nasty type of student. Also the resisting student. I also fear a student who might say, "You haven't helped me at all, what a waste of time talking to you has been."
- The kinds of people I prefer to help are students who are less fortunate. Kids who come from financially unstable and dysfunctional families.
- I am afraid that I might miss something a student is going through or make the wrong decision in getting him or her help. I also fear that I am a bit gullible at times and that might cause problems in the future.
- My personal goal in working with others is to allow them to be themselves in front of me. I want them to hear the words and actions they present and allow them the space to evaluate themselves and decisions based on their lives.
- I gravitate toward women, men, adolescents, and young adults who are left out of the mainstream and victims.
- My family has had bad experiences with counseling so their opinion is not always favorable. A family member often accuses me of

trying to counsel her when she doesn't want it. But there are other times she does appreciate my listening skills.

- I don't have any experience with issues such as suicide or grief. These topics intimidate me.
- The kinds of problems that interest me are loss and loneliness. I tend to avoid adults who have committed abusive acts and are alcoholics.
- I don't have much patience for the attention seekers who act out of anger and have a tendency to display cruel and vindictive behavior. Yes, I am sure that I sometimes show my indifference to their pleas for attention.
- I am interested in marital problems and blended family issues.
- I guess I would have problems with extramarital affairs. I think I would have a big problem with counseling the "cheater." I feel it's the ultimate betrayal.
- A fear that I have is becoming emotionally involved with my students. Throughout my work experience I have made a conscious effort to maintain a certain level of emotional boundaries.
- I hope that I can conceal my uneasiness in a counseling relationship until I can consult with another professional or tell the client how I am feeling in an appropriate way.
- I have a strong interest in broken homes due to divorce, single parenthood, anger, loneliness, academic and peer struggles, and abuse.
- My counselor at my school was not there for me. I wasn't as outgoing as some other students and my counselor seemed to only want to help those students.
- My "I don't want to deal with it list" would probably include teenage pregnancy because I've never dealt with it before.
- I tend to gravitate toward needy people. In college I was often referred to as the mother of the group, always helping or being asked.
- A fear for me in the counseling process is a death of a student, parent, or teacher.
- In terms of helping, I gravitate toward teenagers. I can handle what they dish out, for the most part. I don't have patience for adults, therefore, I avoid them.

- I tend to gravitate toward the isolated students who look like they need help. But I know that the popular students or overachievers also have many problems that are more difficult to observe and need help.
- I have experienced a great deal in my life and feel it could be an asset. There have been many deaths in my family. I have lived through alcoholism and recovery and serious illness (of family members).
- At times, I am too sensitive, a bit judgmental, and tend to want to give advice.
- My family members have watched me move forward from an abusive marriage, divorce, and single parenthood, to being self-supporting and able to stand confidently on my own. They have commended me many times. I am grateful for that.
- I think I have a problem counseling people who are lazy or not hard working. I also have a problem with students who are mean to other students, and that is something that might come through.
- I have a great interest in suicide right now but I am somewhat fearful of handling it due to my own issues.
- I can remember going through middle school and high school being confused and making some bad choices. I don't think there was anyone I could talk to.
- I think my biggest problem will be avoiding my own past problems and how they may affect me.
- I like to help middle and high school level students. I like working with both boys and girls, probably girls better. I like the well-educated but probably more of the not-so-well-educated.
- I want to be the kind of counselor kids come back to visit.
- I may have a tough time counseling victims. I need practice. I don't know what to do with them.
- I tend to favor the underdog.
- I prefer to help with problems of abuse, loss, and loneliness and kids who are brought up by one parent. I prefer not to help someone who thinks they are superior to other people.

The concerns, need for more training, and comfort-level issues raised in this sample of potential helpers provide important data for training leaders of counseling groups. This data helps identify the issues that may be important to future leaders in providing them with ongoing training that can prepare them for a group leadership role. It's a simple but necessary intervention plan so the novice counselor can consider what is required in this new role, develop some beginning skills, and know the resources available for additional training and support.

Finally, the inventory serves the valuable purpose of helping novice helpers remember those adults who helped them to resolve personal problems in their own teen years. These were often adults who played a central role in their lives as teachers, coaches, or other school personnel. The adults saw them every day, knew them well, and made themselves available when trouble came their way.

The inventory helps novice group leaders recall the welcoming words and behaviors of these caring individuals and how their overtures were successful in helping them. Now they are able to recall the mentors and helping models in their own pasts that were instrumental in teaching them a great deal about how help is given.

The inventory also offers them the opportunity to recall those adults who seemed uncaring or remote and who were clearly not interested in offering an open door to help. We did indeed learn much in our teen years, both from those who invited us in and from those who closed their doors to us. We know what works and what doesn't because of our own experience.

Many group leaders have experienced troubles along the path to adulthood. It is important to help them remember that there were important lessons learned from having troubles, having someone help them, and regaining their confidence in the process.

It is also important for novice helpers to remind themselves that counselors are human. Perhaps some of the potential helpers who failed to offer help to them as teenagers were caring people but were overextended in their own personal and professional lives. They may have wanted to help but were trapped in a bureaucratic role and/or personal crises. Helpers can't always deliver help and that is why we need many of them available, to step in when one fails. Many open doors for help work better than just a few.

STEP SIX: TRAINING POTENTIAL GROUP LEADERS TO REFLECT ON THEIR PERSONAL AND PROFESSIONAL INVOLVEMENTS WITH ISSUES THAT STUDENTS OFTEN BRING INTO GROUP COUNSELING SESSIONS

These final reflections can serve to help group leaders become more aware that they are not immune to the same problems affecting their students. They are connected and bound together by the good and bad that life offers each human being.

The stories of troubled lives, surviving, and hope for change as told by students are often stories the group leader knows well. His own personal experience needs to serve as a reminder that his role as group leader is not a distant, teacher-lecturer role but rather one of a wise mentor who has walked the talk. He has been or will be in their shoes. Here are examples of the issues that many group leaders have experienced that are often present in their students' lives:

- Being welcomed and accepted.
- Problematic issues they are trying to resolve.
- Death, loss, and bereavement.
- Thoughts of suicide.
- Saying goodbye and moving on when it is necessary.
- Issues around sexual orientation.
- The place of failure in students' lives.
- Fighting the demons of alcohol.
- Coming to grips with eating disorders.
- Living with an ongoing lack of success in one's personal and school life.
- Trying to fight off the hurtful labels that keep coming your way.
- Aging too fast as a teen because of academic demands and feelings that unless you persist you'll miss your chance.
- The perils of parents separating and divorcing for teens.
- Using/abusing "good grade" pills to succeed.

Here are a series of reflections to help group leaders in training focus more intensely on the above issues and how they may have impacted them personally and professionally.

- Reflection on "being welcomed and accepted into a group or, conversely, being rejected and isolated."

    Simply put, are we made to feel we are "in the club" or somehow less valued? This topic is very real for us as individuals and group leaders. When we enter a new group do we feel welcomed, a part of what's about to happen, or on the outside looking in? We will start with a short written reflection of how we have felt being welcomed, or not welcomed, as is often the case, into a new situation such as school, graduate course, club, family, job, relationship, organization, church, etc. Focus on one experience that was either helpful or hurtful and had some important life lessons for you.

- Reflection on "one problematic issue we have tried to resolve in our present and/or past life." We all arrive here having had a life experience in which we had to work hard to resolve problems. We've learned some important skills through rough times, skills that stand us in good stead for the next rounds of problems we know will come our way. Focus on one problematic area that had some important lessons for you.

- Reflection on death, loss, bereavement, and grieving. Death and loss are a major part of our lives. Some of our loved ones, colleagues, friends, and even our students and their parents have become ill and slowly drifted into despair and death. Others die unexpectedly from an accident, a sudden stroke, even suicide. We are all touched by death. Time stands still. We feel mixed emotions of loss, anger, and despair.

    As counselors our professional role often requires coming to the aid of those impacted by death and helping them prepare for the wake and funeral and focus on what to say, how to hold oneself together, how to have some hope amid such sorrow. But we are also affected on a personal level when death comes calling. We too feel a sense of our own vulnerability and that our clock is ticking away as well. Focus on one experience with death and loss that had a great impact on you and provided some important lessons for life.

- Reflection on suicide. Suicide and suicidal thoughts are no strangers to us on a personal and professional level. We all can reach a point when it becomes difficult to go on, difficult to keep trying to get over the mountain we are climbing and find relief and peace. Most of us find ways to fend off such inner thoughts and go on. But others seem helpless. Yet in most cases these at-risk people send signals and leave messages asking for help that in a curious way often go unnoticed.

Lay people often think they are "unqualified" or that "it's not my role" to reach out to a person who speaks about suicide. Some professionals also feel "unqualified" and think it's not their role, their specialty. Their door is not open when it comes to suicide issues. What has been your experience with suicide issues? Are you prepared to be a source of help in this area? What concerns do you have? Focus on one aspect of suicide, either personal or professional, that concerns you.

- Reflection on saying goodbye, moving on, and finding your way. Here again we find ourselves on familiar ground. Each of us, since childhood, has chosen, for various reasons, to end relationships, say goodbye, and move on to find the space that is uniquely ours. We've had to dodge and reject the will and advice of well-intentioned parents, family members, friends, siblings, counselors, teachers, pastors, supervisors, etc., who wanted us to become "their vision" for us. Simply put, become what they wanted, not what we wanted.

  Like most of our students we too had to learn how to say no, to state "this is what I need; this is the road I'm taking." Focus on one experience in your life when you had to take the road less traveled and turn your back on those who would have had you do otherwise. How did this decision change you and your relationships with these significant others?

- Reflection on sexual orientation. Developing a sexual identity is a key developmental task in adolescence and this identity can change with time and experience. Many self-identified adults knew they were homosexual, lesbian, or bisexual as preteens in elementary school and as teenagers in junior high and high school.

  And often as preteens, teenagers, and young adults they are victims of open hostility and rejection; they are often forced to the margins of community life and at risk of committing suicide. Forced isolation and anonymity has its costs and dark side. What has been your experience as a professional and as a person with this issue? Are you prepared to offer counsel to gay, lesbian, and bisexual students? What are your concerns? Focus on one personal and/or professional experience you've had in this area.

- Reflection on failure. Failure is very much a part of our lives. We experience failure in many ways, in relationships with parents, wives, husbands, partners, friends, and school, work, and in our own negative personal assessment of our self-worth. In developing as a person hopefully we learn how to move on from failure experiences and ready ourselves for the next challenge that will be coming our way, better prepared by learning important life lessons and skills from these past and hurtful failures.

   Many of our students arrive at our door having been hit hard emotionally by failures in their personal, family, and school lives, sometimes in all three areas. As a counselor you can sense their heavy hearts and the bad news they carry with them. Their failure story is written all over them, in their eyes, body stance, and voice. This voice can be silenced or loud, raging, and angry because of experiencing too many bad days and failures.

   What has been your personal experience with failure? What important life lessons did you learn from these experiences? Focus on one failure experience that seemed to hit you hard.

- Reflection on alcohol use and abuse. Those of us who drink alcohol know that the stuff works to tune out life's stresses and problems. But many of us also know that alcohol can have its downside and lead to using alcohol to help solve problems, irresponsible personal and professional behavior, poor health, sexual dysfunction, abuse and violence, even death. Some of us have developed this awareness through tough experiences with alcoholic parents, partners, siblings, friends, co-workers, and our own personal struggle.

   Many students bring issues related to alcohol and its damaging impact on their family and peer relationships. What has been your experience with the impact of alcohol on family members, friends, colleagues, and yourself? Are you ready and set to counsel students in this area? Focus on one life experience you've had in relationship to alcohol use and abuse.

- Reflection on eating disorders. Eating disorders such as bulimia, anorexia, and obesity visit many children and teenagers in our schools. In most cases these disorders are very visible to teachers, counselors, coaches, support staff, and administrators who have daily contact with students. These disorders have a high fatality rate and are the root of many health problems. School can help prevent many of these disorders by early detection and intervention by skilled educators, but it is a challenging mission.

For example, the pressure to "look thin" consumes our school culture. Diets, working out, and taking diet pills and supplements are a way of life for many students who are often high achievers and star athletes. The culture of "thin" has targeted secondary school students, particularly young women, as their most sought-after clients. And student obesity is often fueled by poverty and a daily diet that raises the risk of serious illness.

Having students change their behaviors is not an easy task and sometimes, as in the case of obesity, it is controlled by forces outside the reach of the school. But change can begin with small, incremental steps. Students can participate in counseling groups where they can speak their concerns, take action steps, get the support of their peers, and find helping resources in the community.

What has been your experience with eating disorders? How has this issue affected your family, friends, etc? Focus on one experience you have had with this issue.

- Reflection on success. Many students come into groups with little awareness of their successes. Because success is so often correlated with high grades, athletic achievements, and honors won, many students do not view themselves as successful. They go to school, pass courses, and do what's required, but they are never in the top tier and know they never will be. They live a life that in their eyes is not much to brag about. They think of themselves as average or below average in the big scheme of things.

Often one of our priorities as group leaders is to hear their stories and help them search for successes in their lives. Presenting them with a gift that says, "Whoa, you have done some good things in your personal and school life; make a list and don't lose it." Maybe small things they've done well like write an excellent book report, excel in a work experience, be a big brother or sister to impoverished kids, move out of a damaging relationship, overcome an alcohol, drug, or tobacco addiction, overcome a serious illness, help an aging grandparent, be supportive and helpful to others, or be the first in their family to make it through high school and consider going to college.

Our role as counselors is to help students open up those dimly lit windows, remember when they felt successful, and somehow feel those feelings again, make them their "friends," and begin to talk about how to feel them again and share them with others. What has been your experience with success? Are you, like many of your students, in denial about all of your accomplishments?

Is it easier for you to focus on others' successes and stay in the background, not shining your light at family and professional gatherings? Are you standing by while your family gloats over Uncle Joe for his recent law degree, your successes as a student, educator, counselor, husband, wife, friend, father, etc., staying hidden? Do you find sharing your successes to be easy or difficult, or does that sharing simply never happen? Reflect on your successes and be prepared to share them. Now's your chance!

- Reflection on labeling. Many students seek help trying to shake off hurtful labels that they have acquired in childhood and as teens. Settings like homes, schools, athletic teams, clubs, and church groups are supposed to be helpful and nourishing but they can be hostile and abusive places. They can be places where some kids are assaulted and abused with negative labels that can sting, embarrass, hurt, and create self-doubt.

  You've heard some of these labels, maybe this past week, maybe even been called them yourself. Here are a few examples: lazy, underachiever, heavyset, too fat, too thin, faggot, too bright, a loner, hangs with the wrong crowd, queer, doesn't work up to potential, not prepared, doesn't participate, two-time loser, nigger, not worth saving, homo, troubled, explosive, stoned, dirtbag, druggie, nerd, screwed-up family, sure to keep making the same mistakes, and ass-kisser.

  What has been your personal experience with being labeled by family members, classmates, peers, teachers, coaches, professors, so-called friends, co-workers, etc? Can you still hear their voices? Write about one incident that still hurts.

- Reflection on aging. Aging is an issue for many people regardless of chronological age. For example, many overachieving children and teens feel they have to secure a certain number of academic achievements by a certain age and grade in order to get into the best colleges. This is also true for children and teens that are gifted in music, the arts, athletics, etc. They too feel they have to reach a performance level by a certain age in order to qualify for scholarships.

  Conversely, children and teens who encounter personal and academic setbacks often feel they have "missed their chance," that they can never make it back to the mainstream, and that they are lifetime losers. What has been your personal experience with the expectations that surround the aging process?

- Reflection on divorce and separation. Divorce and separation issues and problems are all around us. Family members, friends, co-workers, and even we have been involved in the tough world of divorce. Many of us know from firsthand experience the hard fact that in the divorce process our lives can change dramatically. There are few winners and children often bear the brunt of a failed marriage. We can lose our family, home, income, health benefits, neighbors, and friends over a few months' time. And we can lose our hopes, dreams, spirit, and health in the process.

  There are, as we all know, few amicable divorces. Divorce courts and lawyers carrying your story in their briefcases can be intimidating. And poor decisions about finances can bring long-term negative consequences. Where does one turn for the best advice and counsel? Who among family members and friends is to be trusted? And often the will and skills needed to fight for "our fair share" don't come easily for unprepared, naive, and innocent victims of divorce.

  In our counseling work we come face to face with many children, teens, and parents careening, tumbling through a divorce that often takes many years. And once that process ends it is followed by the new challenges of how to create a new life and find caring relationships. What has been your experience with divorce? Focus on one particular experience you've had with this issue as a child, teen, or adult.

- Reflection on the use and abuse of "good grade pills." More and more high-achieving students are abusing prescription stimulants due to the pressure of grades and competition for college admissions. Pills that were once found only on college campuses and in graduate school have became a staple for the best and brightest high school students in order to stay number one, be the standard bearers for their class.

  School counselors, nurses, and community health, mental health, religious, and law enforcement organizations are sounding the alarm about the dangers involved in such pills as Adderall. Adderall is an amphetamine prescribed for attention disorders which students are using to study late into the night, focus during tests, and get the good grades they need to get into the best colleges and universities and make their parents and school proud. The "good grade pill" problem appears to be more rampant in wealthy communities where there is great pressure on students to gain admission into Ivy League colleges.

  Counselors planning group counseling intervention need to consider involving the best and brightest students in their school in groups so they can have a safe place, an outlet, from the pressures they may be experiencing from their peers, parents, and school and community leaders who see these standard bearers as a brand name to sell the successes of their school to the community.

  What has been your experience with the downside that can come when high-achieving students are used as a tool, a brand name, a product, to promote their school? In your role as counselor are you ready to advocate for ways to reduce the academic and personal pressures on high-achieving students even if your actions are seen by some critics, administrators, colleagues, and parents as an attempt to lower academic standards? In some high-pressured schools, advocating for students can have its career risks.

  Finally, have your own successes as a student been used to highlight your school's successes rather than your personal achievements?

This series of training activities will hopefully provide potential group leaders and administrators with a philosophy, framework, and path ahead to guide them as they move into the real world of offering groups. That is to do their best, be ready and set, to enter the world of their students and be seen as caring and honest people who have the promise to help them with their struggles and find their way, go on. No, not miracle workers or messiahs who can quickly make them well, happy, and cared for, but rather people who are choosing to give their best effort to understand some of the stresses the students are experiencing, sort them out, and help them find "their" path, not abandon them in this time of need.

They must be prepared to be strong, tough, and capable, up to the task of hearing the stories of students no matter how hurtful, confusing, and unsettling they may be and how hard it is for them to share with others. A counselor who is able to communicate to students that he too has been in some of the distress they are experiencing and that he understands how stressful life can be when there seems to be no one in your corner to help.

Administrators and group leaders will know if they have the right counselor for this important task when they walk the halls of the school, sit in the cafeteria, and hear the voices of group members talking positively about their group experience. Here's an example:

> Maybe you should think about joining Ms. Foley's group. I have been in it since October and it has really helped me. But believe me being a member of her group is not easy. She has a way of getting each of us, there are twelve members, to talk about our lives and what's going wrong and right. Foley doesn't just let you sit there and not get involved. She has a way of expecting us to talk about our problems and help each other. It's like that's our job.
>
> She listens a lot and actually doesn't say much. But Foley can be tough and confront us when she thinks we are pulling back and not giving our all. And she's not afraid to touch on sensitive topics. I know you've been having trouble at home and your Dad was arrested for abusing your sister. It's no secret, all the kids know, so you need to stop trying to hide what is happening to you. We learn in the group it's okay to let others know what is going on, particularly those who can help you.
>
> Foley is one of those people. She understands the kind of stuff that's going on with your family. She's not like some of the other teachers who don't know shit about life or what kids go through. And best of all Ms. Foley keeps what we say private and warns us we'd

better do the same. She says what goes on here stays here. And I know she is for real because I never hear anything about what goes on in our group. I hope you decide to join our group. It might be very helpful. It has been for me. If you'd like I can make an appointment with Ms. Foley for both of us. You learn in the group how to help others, not just yourself.

KEY IDEAS

- In our training with aspiring group leaders we need to be on the lookout for the Ms. Foleys of the world. They arrive with a unique talent and a persona that says "I am made for this work." They are like a raw but very talented athlete, actor, musician, writer, teacher, or politician, whose very presence suggests the potential for the kind of group leader and counselor every student and parent needs. The excitement that comes with training counselors as group leaders is heightened when we come across the Foleys and find ourselves wanting to give our all to her and help her be the best counselor Foley she can be. There are "natural" counselors and we need to use our training to not let them slip away because every guidance department needs a Ms. Foley to lead them toward helping students.

- The curriculum for training aspiring group leaders follows a similar process for group leaders planning the kinds of groups to be offered to students. The group leader goes out among the students and holds conversations about the issues they are facing and what kinds of groups would be helpful for them. He builds his curriculum and group offerings based on what they need. The trainer for aspiring group leaders needs to follow the same process. He holds individual conversations with each counselor as well as the group as a whole to identify the issues they are concerned with and what kind of training would be helpful to them. In these conversations he is able to interject the kind of training that has worked well with other training groups and queries whether they would be helpful for them. In this process he is inviting each member to be not simply a "student" but rather a valued colleague in the training process. He creates an inclusive environment in which each member is invited to be a full partner, as the training process is about "them" and what "they" need, and in the process he helps them gain confidence, skills, and savvy about the issues that are sure to arise in group work. These include issues that they have thought of, some of which are anxiety-provoking, and some they have not thought about but now need to consider.

- Training counselors goes two ways—not only do the aspiring group leaders need to benefit, but also the trainer. He needs to make it clear to members that they are in this training together and his major goal is to make them ready and set to lead counseling groups. But he reminds them that there is something in this training process for him. For example, he needs to find the right way, the path, to make this training real and helpful for them so they are able to leave more confident, secure, informed, aware of their counseling skills that work, aware of their skills that need improvement, and aware of those whom they can regularly turn to for guidance, advice, and counsel. And he reminds members that in order to accomplish this goal he will model a variety of leadership skills that they will need in their groups. For example, he needs to try to make a positive connection with each member, even those who may be resistant; call on each member to participate and share their concerns; confront those members who sit back, become observers, hide from discussions, and feel they do not need more training; and encourage, motivate, and sometimes push each member to practice leading a group. In other words, members are going to have to put in the necessary work to lead. Some aren't going to like it and they will resist, even take on the trainer, much as some students do in counseling groups. Members will need to be reminded that while they are competent professionals, they are also human and can display some of the negative behaviors students adopt in groups. They will also have to be made aware that they may see themselves in students who display the same behaviors in groups. For example, chronic talkers, dominators, distracters, rescuing members, negative members, resistant members, and hostile members. They will also have to deal with members who are prejudiced, racist, and insensitive, and members who are out to take the leadership away from the trainer. And they will need to be sensitive to the reality that some of the topics in the training may involve a personal crisis they have experienced in the past or that is very much alive in their present life. Problems that students bring into group are often no stranger to a seemingly mature and problem-free group leader. It's helpful for group leaders to remember their humanness, past and present life issues, and vulnerability, and that they are more alike their students than they realize.

- Effective training gives members the opportunity to experience what it is like to sit in the "hot seat" of a group leader. The leadership role involves a series of give and take between group members and between members and the group leader. It's not a teaching, lecturer, or presenter role in which the speaker allows the audience only the control and response he is comfortable with. In groups the leader's goal is to share his leadership role with members and, as a result, control is loosened, set free, and members can learn how to be both an effective leader and a participant. This kind of group activity can be a rough ride for leaders, as many students have had little experience in learning how to trust others, speak or share their thoughts and feelings out loud with others, hear hurtful and negative stories that are similar to their own lives, help others who have lost hope to go on, and get useful feedback, some not easy to hear and accept, on how to go on and find their place. In this place they can be at peace, be useful, loving and loved, happy, at least a few days a week, belong, and have a home which is theirs and where the furniture, flowers, and pictures speak of their lives and journey.
- Group leadership may not be an easy professional path to follow, but it does present a wonderful and unique opportunity to help many students find their place and be safe, accepted, and valued. It's a noble undertaking, surely not one for the faint of heart, but if done right it has many rewards. Who could ask for anything more? Helping kids, doing good, can be as good as it gets.

NOTES

1. William L. Fibkins, "Counselor Sexual Misconduct Awareness Inventory." Unpublished, 2005.

2. William L. Fibkins, "Group Leaders Self-Awareness Inventory." Unpublished, 2007.

6

CONCLUSION

The main question raised in this book is "Is anyone listening?" School organizations can answer that question positively by providing helping groups that can aggressively respond to students who are facing trouble in their personal and academic worlds.

Groups provide a protective shield for these students by offering them a safe place where they can find a respite and sense of belonging, learn they are not alone in their struggle, and find a way out of their troubled lives. Groups provide a barrier to the sorrow and hurt they may be experiencing in their everyday lives.

For many students being invited to participate in a helping group serves as a much-needed lifeline and comes none too soon. Personal problems don't disappear without caring intervention; they only get worse.

Schools, after all, are not filled with students who are well cared for and happy. Some may appear that way, but their appearance may cover other problems that they are trained not to reveal. Sending a message that you need help doesn't come easily for many students, particularly high achievers who are groomed to succeed at all costs.

Students who act out and are known in the school as discipline problems, bullies, and dropout material, who spend the majority of their school life in detention rooms or being suspended and are chronic abusers of tobacco, alcohol, and drugs, are often more able to get the help they need. Their acting out makes noise and draws the attention of school administrators and counselors. Making lots of noise is a good way for troubled teens to have their voices heard.

But bad things can happen to any student in the school, not just the ones who act out. The so-called quiet, well-behaved, bright, and seemingly problem-free kids can also get hit hard but sometimes no one is watching them, taking note of their difficulties, and offering an invitation to help.

Effective group counselors are aware of how various groups in the school present or hide their problems. They understand every student can be at risk at some point and know where the open doors for help are in the school. Trouble can arrive unexpectedly. For example, parents get divorced, close relatives die, kids get bullied and fail, addictions to tobacco, alcohol, and drugs take over, suicide becomes a possibility as a result of too much peer rejection, and immigrant students can't find their way in the new world

The list doesn't stop there. High-achieving students get addicted to "good grade pills" such as Adderall, an amphetamine, in order to study late into the night, focus during tests, and get the grades they need to get into the best colleges; female students diet to the extreme and become anorexic or bulimic; star student athletes can't keep up with the pressure that comes with stardom; and some students get lost in our large high schools and anomie becomes a way of life. Many of our large high schools have a student population of over 2,500 students.

Groups provide an open door for these students to find help. Groups are an important part of a circle of wellness that provides secure places where troubled students are welcomed and cared for. Groups and group leaders who are well-known to troubled students and caring staff serve as an antenna and a welcoming light in the fog that often surrounds students in trouble. A place they can feel safe at last.

Schools that offer group counseling intervention are being proactive and doing what is necessary to make sure their public relations promise of not allowing one student to fall between the cracks is not simply a publication relations gimmick. Counselors in these forward-looking schools are not waiting in their offices for troubled students to show up. They are out and about on the frontlines of the school, establishing outposts such as counseling groups to engage students in need of support.

For example, crisis support groups that may be needed for students because of an unforeseen crisis such as the sudden death of a student, parent, or favorite teacher and ongoing support groups as described in chapter 3 are needed to address the ongoing personal, academic, and well-being problems of students.

Groups that respond to a crisis and groups that respond to the everyday pressing problems of students are both needed interventions in an effective outreach program manned by well-trained counselors who have earned a reputation as first responders. These counselors know they need to be tuned in to the daily events in their school that may require speedy intervention using both counseling groups and individual counseling.

Establishing counseling groups, supported with a one-on-one counseling backup resource, is a critical addition in an effort to create a circle of wellness to address student problems. But it is only one part of the effort. In an effective guidance and counseling program leaders of counseling groups are also involved in a parallel outreach effort to train teachers, administrators, students, support staff, and parents to be advisers and helpers. They can serve as creditable sources of referral to school and community health and mental health professionals and become partners in the circle of wellness.

For far too long, secondary school guidance and counseling has been strong on offering guidance services and weak on establishing counseling interventions such as groups to help student resolve their personal problems and training members of the staff, students, and parents to be helpers when they observe a student headed for trouble.

Counselors have been stuck in a quasi-administrative role that focuses on guidance activities such as scheduling students for classes, leading mandated testing programs, guiding students for college admissions and scholarships, and taking on administrative duties such as discipline and monitoring student attendance. These interventions may leave students with personal problems asking, "Is anyone listening?"

We need to put the word "counseling" back into the mission of guidance and counseling departments. In many schools counseling interventions have gotten lost along the way and resulted in many troubled students getting lost along the way as well. And so have many gifted personal counselors who could find no role in a guidance-oriented department.

Is anyone listening? Here are some possible choices as described in a conversation between a veteran counselor and a novice counselor who has just entered the profession. Which counselor behaviors represent the counseling model we want to follow as a profession?

Two counselors are leaving the school building heading home. One was an older man who had been a counselor in the school for thirty years. He appeared energetic and full of life. The other was a young woman who was in her first year as a counselor at the school. She appeared disheveled and tired. As they walked out of the school, the young woman asked the supposedly wise older counselor how he managed to look so full of life after listening to students all day. The older counselor's reply was "Who listens?"

This book is a follow-up of the author's book *Wake Up, Counselors: Restoring Counseling Services for Troubled Teens*. The book is briefly described in chapter 1. *Wake Up Counselors* focused on two important issues affecting school guidance and counseling programs: the demise of personal counseling in our secondary schools and how these services can be restored by reassigning members of the counseling staff to serve as personal counselors to provide outreach for troubled students

This book takes the needed next step by describing how group counseling can be an important intervention strategy for the personal counselor to help get troubled students on board to resolve their problems, not remain left alone at the margins of school life to figure things out for themselves.

It's time for leaders of guidance and counseling departments to stop lamenting they need more staff to meet the growing needs of troubled students. In this time of limited resources new counselors are not going to be hired in the vast majority of our secondary schools. Directors of guidance and student service administrators need to honestly confront this new normal. It's not 1960 anymore, when counselors were in great demand and hired in droves.

The guidance and counseling profession is now faced with a historical challenge; either it changes course and reorganizes its personal counseling outreach so that it has relevancy to today's students and their problems or it will face a slow death as a major contributor in helping students resolve their personal, academic, and well-being problems.

However, one thing we know about organizational renewal is that organizations tend to stay with what they know, even if it's not working. This is also true for personal relationships. People tend to stay connected to each other even though the bottom is falling out in their lives. What we know has a seeming safety net to it, while ideas for change lay stagnant until the system fails completely. The sentiment, "I should have seen it coming. Why didn't I? The need for change was so clear and why did I keep my blinders on?" often fits the collapse of a troubled organization and personal relationship.

That's sort of what is going on now in the inner circles of the leaders' guidance and counseling departments. No, the system hasn't broken down completely, but there are growing signs, warning lights, that the guidance and counseling model hatched in the 1950s is reaching the point where it can no longer deliver the kinds of personal counseling services needed by today's students, parents, teachers, administrators, and by counselors themselves.

And that warning light is not new. It's been flashing since the student unrests in the early 1970s and growing brighter each year since. Sure, guidance and counseling departments can still deliver on the quasi-administrative services such as college admissions, scheduling for classes, overseeing mandated testing programs, and attendance and discipline interventions. But this is a delivery system that is failing many students. There is little opportunity for counselors to deliver personal counseling services in this system.

The quasi-administrative services listed above get top priority and what has priority gets done. These services also get measured and are used by school administrators to gather and report positive data to demonstrate the school's academic successes and pass school budgets. The counselor's top priority is to keep the positive data flowing to the administration.

Meanwhile personal counseling is usually given a low priority and rarely measured. In the author's experience little data regarding personal counseling interventions is gathered or used to demonstrate the value of counseling interventions in aiding the success of students and the school. What is given a priority and measured gets done. What doesn't gets put on the back burner and has no status or value in the school organization. And that's where personal counseling services and well-trained personal counselors are now finding themselves. When there is no data, it is too easy to conclude there are no student problems or to describe problems with vague generalities.

This should come as no surprise. The vast majority of secondary schools are still organized according to a 1950 model in which counselors are assigned to students by grade or alphabet rather than on the basis of their counseling skills and training. Everyone's lumped together to deliver the quasi-administrative tasks that are required. As a result there's no room for specialties such as skills in group counseling, one-on-one personal counseling, or training educators, students, and parents to be helpers, thereby creating a community of helpers and a circle of wellness.

This book and its predecessor, *Wake Up Counselors*, offer a new model for guidance and counseling services, a model in which counseling services can become a reality for troubled teens rather than a meaningless sign on a counselor's door. If the current system is not changed not only will students continue to lose out, but so will caring counselors who understand they are trapped in a system which is putting their profession at risk.

Hopefully it will provide a guide and encouragement for counselors to advocate for the changes that need to be made, to, like their troubled students, find their voices and be heard. However the path for change will be difficult. The pressure on counselors from directors of college admission programs and many school district administrators to stay with the 1950 counseling model which views the counselor role as the gatherer-in-chief of positive data is real.

College admission directors want counselors focused on getting students into their colleges, not doing personal counseling. Counselors are the main resource to keep college enrollments up, especially for colleges without a national name and student following. And many school district administrators want counselors focused on gathering positive data, not doing personal counseling. Counselors are the main resource enabling them to bring "good news" to the community and votes for school budgets. Efforts to bring personal counseling on board by reorganizing guidance and counseling services will be resisted by those who rely on counselors to help make their jobs successful.

The answer, the way to proceed, is to reorganize guidance and counseling services so that there are two tiers. For example, tier one, in which the majority of the counseling staff deliver quasi-administrative guidance activities, and tier two, in which one or two counselors, depending on the size of the school, deliver personal counseling services such as group counseling, one-on-one personal counseling, and training for students, parents, support staff, teachers, and administrators.

Change is possible if we are creative enough to help those who resist change to visualize how it can come about, see it as doable, and appreciate its value to the guidance and counseling service and to the entire school community. Counselors committed to change need to engage and get the attention of those in power to support the kinds of changes this book recommends. That is, sell them on the needed change by helping them see that there is something good in the proposed change for them as well as the entire school community.

However, it is important to remember that the value of a good idea for changing an organization is not in its origin but in its delivery. Therefore leaders of group counseling programs need to make sure the program is actually working to respond to the personal and academic needs of students that are being promised on paper or after a burst of early success is allowed to die out because of a change of leadership, a lack of support, or unfounded criticism that damages the integrity of the program. Ongoing assessments and keeping close ties with key supporters are critical to the survival of any school reform. Leaders of group counseling programs need to be in relationships with many members of the school community. They live and survive in a world which is interdependent and need to take care of the roots that helped establish the program. Attention must be paid to supporters as well as students. A saying in the world of sports says it all, "you go to the dance with the players who brought you there."

Change is all about taking action, doing, and as the needed change takes hold, being able to abandon those aspects of the program that are not working well and reinforcing those program elements that are working well. It's a process fraught with risks, but in the case of student groups it is worth doing. Change may be risky for many reasons. For example it could result in failure, of the program and of the professional career dreams placed on hold by the leader. But change can also prove to be life-giving, an exhilarating experience, an opportunity for renewal, a rescue from a deadened career and a job that has become tiresome and boring.

If change is the road not taken by guidance programs and counselors, it may seem easier and produce less conflict to stand pat, to keep asking and waiting for more counseling staff, and to hope for change to somehow magically happen. But standing pat and settling is often a prescription for failure. That's true in both the professional and personal arena. If this path is taken, counselors are like their troubled students who do nothing about their problems, who don't ask for or seek help, turn a blind eye to their troubles, and accept life as it is. Meanwhile they are moving closer and closer to living a life at the margin.

Which path are the school district administrators of student services, directors of guidance and counseling departments, and their counselors going to choose? Are they listening?

REFERENCES

Bowers, Judy, Trish Hatch, and American School Counselor Association. *The ASCA National Model: A Framework for School Counseling Programs*. Alexandria, VA: American School Counselor Association, 2005.

College Board. *Counseling at the Crossroads*. National Office of School Counseling Advocacy, 2011.

Fibkins, William L. *Class Warfare: Focus on "Good" Students Is Ruining Schools*. Lanham, MD: Rowman & Littlefield, 2013.

———. Counselor Sexual Misconduct Awareness Inventory. Unpublished, 2005.

———. Group Leaders Self-Awareness Inventory. Unpublished, 2007.

———. "How to Start a Group Counseling Program." *Student Assistance Journal*, September/October 1994.

———. "Teens + School + Alcohol = Mandatory Counseling." *Student Assistance Journal*, March/April 1995.

———. *Wake Up, Counselors: Restoring Counseling Services for Troubled Teens*. Lanham, MD: Rowman & Littlefield, 2013.

Jacobs, Ed E., Robert L. Masson, and Riley L. Harvill. *Group Counseling Strategies and Skills*. Pacific Grove, CA: Brook/Cole, 2002.

Moore, Budd A. "The Efficacy of Group Counseling Interventions Employing Short-Term Rational Emotive Behavior Therapy in Altering Beliefs and Behaviors of At-Risk Adolescents." Dissertation, Virginia Polytechnic Institute (Virginia Tech), 1999.

Sinclair, Robert L., and Ward J. Ghory. "Last Things First: Realizing Equality by Improving Conditions for Marginal Students." In *Access in Knowledge: An Agenda for Our Nation's Schools*, edited by John Goodlad and Pamela Keating. New York: College Entrance Examination Board, 1990.

www.ingramcontent.com/pod-product-compliance
Lightning Source LLC
Chambersburg PA
CBHW030655270326
41929CB00007B/371